Meditative Flute

Learn how to play the Native American flute to enhance your Yoga, Meditation, Biking, Walk/Run, Pilates, Tai Chi, Workout, or Feldenkrais practice

Dick Claassen

Published by FluteFlights.com
ISBN: 978-1478311768

DEDICATION

I dedicate this book to all those who
want to find their own kind of music and
their own measure of peace. In the words of
American poet, Oliver Wendell Holmes:
"Alas for those that never sing,
but die with all their music in them!"

CONTENTS

~ACKNOWLEDGEMENTS~

None of us work in a vacuum. We all have family and friends who influence the decisions we make and the paths we take. I have a good friend who has a direct influence on my musical life. His name is Chris Fuqua, builder of beautiful bamboo Native American flutes, and weaver of mystical, mythical notes on the flute that will take you to places you'd never think possible. It's Chris's flutes and his constant encouragement that has led me down this joyous path. Chris is one of the good guys, and I'm proud to call Chris my friend.

Two of my other good friends, also good guys, are my daughter Gretchen, a gifted cellist, and my sister Connie, a gifted pianist. We are a musical family, and my daughter's and sister's encouragement has played a large and important role in my own musical evolution.

No, we don't work in a vacuum. We work, and love, and play with people who gift us with *their* love, a love that ultimately makes our lives better.

-Intro-

Stuff You Need to Know

SUPPLEMENTARY AUDIO AND VIDEO FILES: This book has complete **tablatures**, (as well as full explanations, when called for), for every tune. If you are a seasoned musician, the tablatures, (tablature is a simple notation for writing music), alone, will be explanation enough. But along with this book are ***85*** FREE MP3 files. Also included is a video file that reveals the secrets of advanced techniques like the bark, the grace note, the trill, etc., techniques that will make you a masterful flute player. The tunes in this book are not electronically generated tunes spawned by computer software. I have composed, tabbed out, played, and then recorded each tune with my own flute playing. That tune you might be frustrated with by studying just the written tablature suddenly becomes crystal clear with the hearing of it. Especially important are those MP3s that are played in the *extemporaneous free-style,* a style that's difficult for beginners of the Native American flute to learn without solid audio models to emulate. These audio/video files will help you learn to play the flute in this meditative free-style way, just as I do.

WHERE ARE THE FREE FILES? The URL that takes you to the download page for all the *free audio and video files* is at the end of this book. The files are zipped for download, but can be easily unzipped, (double-click to unzip), by both Macs and PCs. (Macs and PCs require no additional zipping/unzipping utility software for this set of files.)

Once you unzip them you can put them anywhere you like and play them in the music management software, (like iTunes or Windows Media Player), that came with your computer, or play them on any mobile device like the iPod, iPhone, Android phone, iPad, Kindle Fire, B&N Nook, or any other tablet.

Since all the files are downloadable, delivery to your hard drive is mere moments away.

~A Quik Hint~

HINT: Clearing the flute of accumulated moisture: If you are new to the Native American flute, you will need this information before you begin. All brass wind instruments have *spit valves.* The curved tubing indicative of this type of instrument traps spit, and periodically this has to be cleared by opening its spit valve and blowing sharply and abruptly to blow it out. The Native American flute has no curved brass tubing, but the design of the blowing end will nevertheless trap spit. Since there is no spit valve on a Native American flute, we clear the airway by doing the following—

1. With the flute horizontal, turn it over so the note holes are at the bottom. (Roll until the note holes face the floor.)

2. Blow sharply and strongly into the blowing end. The spit will clear. It may take more than one blow, but two or three good blows will clear it.

As you play, if the quality of the tone begins to alter at all, clear it as described above. Some flutes require frequent clearing, while others don't require it as often. When the sound quality goes, you'll know it's time to clear the flute.

-Chapter 1-

All About Flutes

WHAT FLUTE IS BEST FOR YOU: There are many different types of Native American flutes, and all these types can be confusing—especially if you are new to the flute. So it will be helpful to be armed with some facts before buying your flute, even if you already have one. The first thing you might want to know is where you can purchase a flute. You will have little luck finding one at a standard brick-and-mortar music store. ("Brick-and-mortar" refers to stores existing as physical buildings on the street.) However, there are an astounding number of flute builders that sell their flutes online. In the interest of transparency, the flute builder I recommend, **Chris Fuqua of Windpoem Flutes**, is a good friend of mine. So you can understand why I favor his flutes over all others. But there are many other equally fine flute builders. Just type "Native American flutes" into your favorite search engine and you will be amazed at the number of pages that turn up.

TYPES OF FLUTES: Once you find a builder, you will need hard facts so the purchase you make is an intelligent one. Flutes come in various sizes, various keys, and various materials. But you must be aware of two distinct classes of flutes. The earliest flute type, historically, had just five holes. I'm referring to the Native American flute design most of us are familiar with. This **5-hole** design is still available. The second flute type has **six holes** and is of more recent design, historically. What's the difference between these two designs? The 6-hole flute is superior, musically, to the 5-hole flute. That's because the 5-hole flute has two fewer available notes than the 6-hole flute. Fifteen specific notes can be played on the 6-hole flute, but on the 5-hole flute only 13 notes can be played. This might seem like a minor issue to you, but as a musician I can assure you it's not. The lack of these two notes on the 5-hole flute makes many tunes impossible to play. That's why I wrote this book for the 6-hole flute and not the 5-hole flute. Although I greatly respect the historical value of the 5-hole flute, these two flute types aren't musicially equivalent. **You will need a 6-hole flute for the tunes in this book.**

WHAT FLUTES ARE MADE FROM: The very earliest flutes created by various American Indian tribes were made from the branch of a tree. Wood with a soft core was chosen. A length was cut. That length was usually made equal to the distance from the maker's elbow to the fingertips. There were no standard dimensions back then. Each flute was an individual effort made to the body measurements of the maker, and this pretty much guaranteed that all flutes were unique in size. The tools used to construct a flute were quite crude, too. A hot coal fastened on the end of a stick was used to slowly burn out the center to make a barrel.

It goes without saying that today's flute builders don't use this slow and inaccurate method. We are all experiencing the digital revolution with all its distractions, and that revolution makes us impatient to finish a time consuming and difficult job before we even start it. But the early craftsperson had nothing but time when s/he constructed a flute. Making something and doing it well was a source of pride for the early flute maker. We can just about imagine the care that went into the construction of this instrument. After the barrel was completed, note holes were drilled, the blowing end was constructed, and the block was carved, much like today's flute builders might do. But burning out the barrel took a very long time. (Thanks to C.S. Fuqua for the early construction method information on the Native American flute.)

BAMBOO FLUTES: Since bamboo is native to many parts of the United States, eventually bamboo was sometimes used rather than wood from a solid tree branch. No more hot coals on the end of sticks! The barrel was premade by nature because bamboo is already hollow. But bamboo also has its own kind of sound that's quite distinctive from the sound of wood, and so bamboo eventually caught on in the flute world.

PVC FLUTES, A MODERN SLANT: A modern material is now used for flutes. It's called PVC—polyvinyl chloride. The name sounds quite chemical, which it is. But this high quality plastic has a gorgeous tone when it's fashioned into a Native American flute. If you are new to the flute, a good PVC flute is an excellent starter instrument. It's also the least expensive flute.

TONE CHARACTERISTICS OF THE THREE FLUTE TYPES: Probably the most popular flute type is the wood flute. Cedar is especially popular. It delivers a sweet tone that many players prefer. Personally I like the bamboo flute for overall tone. To me the bamboo flute has a greater tonal color range. Given the variety of tune types I demand from my flute, I need a flute that can sound both rough and sweet when I want it to. But don't underestimate the PVC flute. It doesn't have the wide tone color spectrum that bamboo does, but these flutes nevertheless have a sweet and very stable tone. They are also easy to finger and deliver a clean note because the hi tech plastic allows for a cleanly bored note hole. This helps eliminate air leaks, which will lead to squeaks and squawks.

PRICE DIFFERENCES OF THE THREE FLUTE TYPES: Usually the standard wood flute is the most expensive. Modern construction methods require the flute body blank to be sawed in half, (sawed lengthwise). It takes considerable time to hollow out both halves and then glue them back together to make the barrel. But the bamboo flute is already a barrel since that's the way bamboo grows. Bamboo grows like a tube, so less time is required to build a high quality flute. The PVC flute made from a near perfect tube, dimensionally, is the least expensive to construct. Yet, this material will give great tone. And the PVC flute is by far the least expensive flute to build. So if you want to experiment with different flute KEYS, the PVC flute is the ideal instrument because it won't break your financial back to buy a few different flutes, all in different keys, so you can experiment.

WHAT ARE FLUTE *KEYS?* Picture yourself sitting at a piano, or an electronic keyboard. You are going to play the song, "Michael Row the Boat Ashore". To do this you press any key for the starting note and begin playing the tune. Now you decide to play it again, but this time you start playing the melody on a DIFFERENT KEY. The melody will still be the same, but it won't be in the same "key" as the previous tune. One melody will sound higher than the other. This is what we mean by different keys. Every wind instrument, regardless of how sophisticated it might be, is made to be in a specific key. And regardless of the instrument, tunes are easiest to play in the key the instrument is in. If we are playing a Bb sax, tunes are easiest to play in the key of Bb. If we are playing a C# Native American flute, tunes are easiest to play in the key of C#. However, we needn't worry about playing in different keys from the tablature. **Tablature is a *relative* notation, not an absolute notation.** All notes are fingered the same on the NA flute, regardless of key. If we want to change the key, we continue to play the tablature with a flute that's in a different key. (Blues harmonica players carry around a case of harmonicas in at least seven different keys.)

ADVANTAGES TO DIFFERENT KEYS: What are the advantages to having flutes in different keys? There are several. If you intend to play with guitar accompaniment, for instance, you will want to use a flute that's in a key like C, D, E, or G. These keys are easiest for hobby guitarists to play in. A flute in the keys of something like F or C# will not make you popular with guitar players. If you plan to entertain the elderly in something like a nursing home setting, you would be better off with lower key flutes like E, Low D, or low C#. A high key flute can be distressing for those who have a hearing loss in specific parts of the frequency spectrum.

PLAYING YOUR FLUTE WITH A FLUTE-PLAYER FRIEND: If you intend to use your flute to play along with another flute player, any key is fine, providing you and your friend are playing flutes that are in the same key. If you intend to play solo, any key will work because you don't have to get along, musically, with the other person. If you are going to play your flute for meditation, you will probably be playing solo. Again, any key is fine. But you might want to stay away from the higher flute keys. A lower key flute is more peaceful.

We are not limited to playing tunes the flute is in. There are several accessible keys on the Native American flute. For example, with just my G flute I can play in the keys of G major and G minor, the keys of C major and C minor, the keys of D major and D minor. There are other keys possible as well, but they require considerable skill to access. Not to worry, though. Although I occasionally play in the more obscure keys, the key "positions" I've named play probably 99% of the tunes you might encounter. We don't explore other keys too much in this book because our sole purpose is to play meditative tunes. But if you are interested in exploring the flute further where you can learn to play in other keys on just one flute, check out my other flute books at FluteFlights.com.

PLAYING EASE: There is a big difference in how builders craft flutes. The first flute I ever bought is beautifully constructed from cedar. But the barrel is long, and a long barrel means the note holes will be proportionally farther apart, which they are. This requires a finger stretch that is nearly beyond me. The flute is in the key of G. When I got my first bamboo flute from Windpoem flutes, Chris surprised me with a shorter barrel and note holes that were easy to reach. Even more impressive was the fact that this flute was in the key of E. The E flute is tuned a step and a half *lower* than my long-barreled G flute. The lower the key, the longer the barrel. But Chris somehow stepped around this problem and delivered a flute with note hole distances I could reach easily, and he did this in a lower key flute. I can't speak for other flute builders, but Chris listens to the customer and builds a flute to accommodate physical limitations the customer might have. If you have arthritic fingers, or if you have a physical disability that limits your reach and strength, Chris will take this into consideration. It's possible that any flute builder will accommodate you with a custom setup. I can't speak for other builders. I only know that Chris will make it work for you, if at all possible.

FLUTES FOR CHILDREN: Playing the flute is a wonderful activity for children. Just be sure you buy them a high key flute. All things being equal, the higher the key, the shorter the barrel. The shorter the barrel, the closer will be the note holes that make it easy for small hands to reach.

ADVANTAGES TO VERY EXPENSIVE FLUTES: Here's a clue: There are no advantages to owning an expensive flute! Not unless appearance and not music is your primary reason for buying a flute. An expensive flute with its hand carved animal block and gorgeous turkey feathers will not sound any better than a flute with a simple but functional block and no turkey feathers. I not only use my flutes to meditate, I use them to play every kind of music imaginable. My expensive flute with its ebony panther block is seldom played. Instead I play my inexpensive bamboo or PVC flutes. They are beautiful flutes in their own right, and they all find a warm and welcoming place in my hand, not on my wall. An expensive block can add as much as a hundred bucks to the final flute price, and that expensive block will not make one iota of difference in the sound of the flute. If you are interested in producing meaningful music, I suggest you forget those expensive add-ons that contribute nothing to the sound.

-Chapter 2-

Different Ways to Meditate

LIFE AND HOW WE LIVE IT: What's your life like? Do you have a perfect life? Is everyone in your family, including you, successful, handsome or beautiful, socially at ease, well behaved, morally perfect, and rich? No doubt there are a few of us out there who feel they do have a perfect life. But they don't. No one does. We all have, in varying degrees, family problems, money problems, marriage problems, problems with school, problems with work, sex problems, problems with staying on the right side of the law, low self esteem, a hot temper, an I-don't-give-a-damn attitude, depression, anxiety, etc., etc., etc. We are human, so by default, we are flawed. Although it's true that "God don't make no junk", our parts are a bit rusty. It was Henry David Thoreau who said: "The mass of men lead lives of quiet desperation." Yes we do. Some of us are so emotionally stressed by our problems that we escape into drugs or alcohol, sometimes both. And if we continue down that path, it's a sure ticket to disaster.

THE POWER OF MEDITATION: When I began to explore meditation in the middle 1970s, great claims were made for it. Meditation, it was purported, would solve ALL of our problems. By practicing meditation we would soon find ourselves in a perfect life. All we had to do was learn how to meditate—for a fee, of course—and before we knew it, life would be very, very good. Wellll...no. Meditation did not miraculously solve my problems, nor anyone else's problems, either. But meditation has made life far easier to bear. A regular practice will take that nasty edge off our lives, and in so doing, our stress level will decrease. And when our stress level decreases, our body's immune system is strengthened. A strong immune system means a healthier life, and a healthier life leads to a new kind of peace. Meditating regularly will help us focus on the task at hand. Those projects you mean to finish but never do will suddenly get finished. Those goals you've set for yourself will finally be met. Meditation gives you a new drive without making you anxious. It will give you a new outlook without changing you. That sunny outlook is in everyone. We just need to learn how to cast out distractions that can take us down the wrong path, and that's what meditation does for us.

You might be wondering if meditation will really make a difference in your life. Maybe I'm just giving you hype. But if you are already meditating, you know it's not hype. If the idea of meditation is new to you, you might want to do a bit of exploring, something I hope this book will help you do. We all do what we do for specific reasons. Those reasons depend upon our interests and talents. Whether we like playing music, playing with paint, or playing a game, we will pursue those interests. So with 7 billion people currently inhabiting our planet, it means our interests and talents are as varied as the infinite number of parallel universes that undoubtedly enfold us. But as humans we all share one common interest, don't we? That interest is to find peace within ourselves. Regardless of our specific personality and interests, we want peace, even if for only a short time. And if we are loving beings, we also will want that peace for those who are close to us.

THE POWER AND GLORY OF YOGA AND OTHER DISCIPLINES: How might we attain this peace? We attain it through a healthy discipline, a discipline we can stick with and enjoy following, a discipline that will help us focus and cast out destructive distractions. This is why the practice of yoga, for example, is so popular. Yoga, and contemplative disciplines like yoga, enable us to follow a specific path in a meditative way, where we can find peace, and eventually find *self awareness,* if self awareness is our ultimate goal. And by the way, yoga doesn't have anything to do with religion. It began its life with the Hindu faith, but the practice itself is generic. All faiths have a long history of contemplative disciplines. This includes Christians, Hindus, Buddhists, Jews, Muslims, and the practitioners of the historical faiths of our Native American brothers and sisters.

BUT ISN'T MEDITATION DANGEROUS? No. Those who say it is are simply frightening people away from a beneficial technique that will improve one's life. Meditation is fully accepted by millions of medical hospitals all over our planet. Every major legitimate place of healing offers meditation as a powerful alternative therapy to control pain and anxiety, as well as promote healing. Unlike powerful pain opiates that can bring on a serious physical and emotional addiction, meditation is not addictive, neither emotionally or physically. Nor does meditation run counter to *any* faith. It's simple to do, *anyone who can think can do it,* and meditating will not open the gates of hell and allow Satan and his mighty army to invade your soul! In this book I give you simple instructions on how to meditate. Whatever your personal faith might be, the men and women in the history of your faith were deep meditators, and they meditated in the same simple ways that are outlined in the meditation instructions in this book. Your Native American flute will help lead you into a meditative state. And the physical poses of yoga will lead you into a meditative state, just as running and Pilates will bring you to that state. There are many ways to find that peace within ourselves, and we will discuss and explore some of those ways.

IS A PHYSICAL ACTIVITY DISCIPLINE SUITABLE FOR EVERYONE? The physical pose side of some of these activities might not be for you. Some people are uncomfortable, for whatever reason, with physical exercise beyond their usual day-to-day activities. Nevertheless, some are determined and will overcome the great limitations they might be physically saddled with. A bright and steadily shining star in the yoga instructor world is Matthew Sanford. Matthew suffered a catastrophic automobile accident when he was a child and was left a quadriplegic where he carries out a good part of his day in a wheelchair. But as a yoga instructor he has risen above these limitations and is recognized as a dynamic instructor, giving inspiration to able bodied and disabled alike. You can learn more about Matthew at matthewsanford.com.

MY PERSONAL MEDITATIVE PRACTICE: Although I have my own physical challenges, I manage a rich, meditative life on several fronts, so you might be interested in my personal meditation practice. I am not your usual "case". I'm a Polio survivor. The Polio virus merrily skips through the brain stem and randomly destroys horn cells at the base of the brain. Horn cells from the brain communicate our physical intention to move, and when a cell is destroyed, it can no longer communicate with those specific muscle bundles in a limb. So we are usually left with at least some use of a limb. But many of the muscle bundles are dormant, leaving movement up to those muscle bundles that can still communicate with the brain. Exercising to improve strength isn't a safe option for a Polio survivor like myself. To physically exert too much would wear out those working muscle bundles we have left. This fact became painfully clear in the 1990's when those Polio survivors who loved to exercise soon found themselves dangerously paralyzed because they had worn themselves out, literally. The medical community didn't fully understand how Polio affected the body back then. Doctors strongly recommended the Polio survivor exercise vigorously, and in so doing, those survivors wore out the remaining muscle bundles long before their time. I tell you all this to emphasize the fact that for some people robust physical exercise can do irreversible damage. A well intentioned yoga, Pilates, or biking regimen can do irreversible damage if you are physically compromised in this way. Know yourself and act accordingly.

FELDENKRAIS, AWARENESS THROUGH MOVEMENT: But this doesn't mean we Polio survivors, or others who might be at risk from doing muscle strengthening exercises, don't have alternatives. Not to be taken down by this disease, I found the perfect alternative for me. It's called, **"Feldenkrais: Awareness Through Movement"**. I do a 30 minute Feldenkrais routine every day. And I mean, every single day without fail. **Feldenkrais is a specialized yoga-like discipline**, and it's perfect for someone like myself who's physically limited in strength. **With Feldenkrais, the object isn't to build muscle, but to increase and maintain flexibility, balance and breath.** In this respect it's like all other yoga-like routines, but with this discipline muscles are not challenged in the practice of it. It's extremely safe, and it has helped me maintain a pain free, healthy body for many years. Like any other mindfully executed discipline, you pay attention to, *(are aware of),* each movement as you perform it, and you breathe with each movement to maximize the benefit of each moving pose. This is a powerful form of meditation and is one of the ways I meditate.

In addition to Feldenkrais, I practice daily a *mantra* meditation. If I find some mornings that I'm restless and have lots of things on my mind, I will at least *begin* my meditation session, even if it's for only 30 seconds, or so. If I don't feel like meditating, I sit down and *start* to meditate anyway, whether I want to or not. That's because *some* meditation is better than *no* meditation. To maintain a steady practice, it's important to meditate every day, even if it's only for a very short time.

If you want to more deeply explore meditation, you might consider my book, Meditation: A Personal Journey, available in both Kindle and print. This book will teach you how to meditate, and it will also give you an inside idea of what meditation is and what it really feels like to meditate. Just go to Amazon.com and type in my name, "Dick Claassen", (without the quotes). It will appear in the list of books I've published through Amazon.

And while I'm on the subject of my published books, you might be interested in my Kindle edition of a 99 cent book titled, Native American Flute DECODED. You'll learn lots of fascinating and useful things about the Native American flute in this inexpensive ebook.

Another excellent book, this one written by my friend, Chris Fuqua, is titled, The Native American Flute: Myth, History, Craft, available in both Kindle and print. This excellent book discusses every aspect of the Native American flute, both past and present. There is even an extensive section that shows you how to build a regular Native American flute as well as how to build the ancient Anasazi end-blown flute. (Talk about a meditative experience!) To find this book, go to Amazon.com and type in Chris's name as "C.S. Fuqua", (without the quotes). You will be met with a list of all the books and stories Chris has written, including the book just mentioned.

Along with Feldenkrais and mantra meditation, I play the Native American flute daily. This greatly augments my regular meditation, and that's what this book is really all about.

THE MEDITATIVE NATIVE AMERICAN FLUTE: People usually think of the Native American flute as an instrument used just for playing traditional Native American music. That's an unfortunate, limited view, because this instrument is capable of delivering any kind of music you might want to play on it. I have written several Native American flute tutorial packages, and in these packages I show the student how to play everything from classical music to the blues, from Christmas carols and venerable old Christian hymns to folk music, from music of other cultures and religions to tunes of romance, and from Native American traditional music to music that will take you into deep meditation. Any and all kinds of music are possible on this beautiful and noble instrument. And this is why I love writing books about the Native American flute.

You are likely reading this book because you practice a mindful physical discipline like yoga, or you practice meditation, (traditionally, meditation is considered to be another form of yoga since the meaning of "yoga" is to *yoke* the mind and the body), or maybe both, and you want to use your Native American flute to enhance your practice. Or you might be curious, wondering how the Native American flute can help you meditate, even if you don't practice any type of mindful discipline.

But this particular instruction book is different than most. This book focuses on the ethereal beauty that comes from the flute when played meditatively. Believe me, writing this book was not an easy project. Before I even began to write this book my first task was to compose tunes that were truly meditative, not just tunes I might knock off with little substance so I could fill up a book. To accomplish this, every morning when the sun was just coming up I sat at my patio door, looking out across my yard. Regardless of the season, I always have birds and bunnies and squirrels in my backyard, and it's peaceful to watch them cavort in the early morning. I keep my bamboo flutes by my patio door, so once I would settle into a morning peace, I would launch the recorder app on my iPhone, pick up my flute, and play meditatively. Later I would listen to my recordings and then *tab them out* so others could play them, too. (We'll get into *tabbed* out tunes later.) Not every tune I recorded was successful, but most were. And it was those successful tunes I eventually put to tablature so you could read the tablature and then play the tunes, just like I can. I eventually rerecorded all the tunes with a high quality digital recorder. Just because I compose a tune on my flute doesn't mean I can remember it. In fact, if I don't record it or tab it out on the spot, chances are I won't remember it. And eventually I need to write down the tune in tablature form so I can play it from the TAB later. That's the real power of tablature; tablature allows us to write down our musical thoughts, just like the alphabet allows us to write down our literary thoughts.

THE FLUTES I PLAY: As already mentioned, the two types of flutes I play are bamboo flutes and PVC flutes made by Chris Fuqua of WindPoem Flutes. These are beautiful sounding flutes, and I play them almost exclusively for all my flute work.

Chris's bamboo flutes are made from naturally downed Alabama bamboo. Most think that bamboo is only native to Eastern countries like Japan and China. But a wide variety of bamboo is grown in different regions of the United States. I especially like bamboo for meditative work because bamboo gives my flutes the sound of the venerable old bamboo end-blown flute called the "shakuhachi" flute. This type of flute comes from Japan and is used by meditating monks as well as by hot jazz players like John Neptune. A bamboo Native American flute gives us that shakuhachi sound without all the heartache and discipline of learning to blow the shakuhachi flute correctly.

Chris's PVC flutes sound ethereal and have a unique ring block that makes adjustment for best tone very simple. (See page 32.) This is a wonderful flute for the novice. And the PVC flute is much less expensive than either a bamboo or wood flute. This inexpensive instrument is a good way to experiment with flutes in different keys without making a significant investment.

If you think you might be interested in Chris's flutes, just go to FluteFlights.com. The WindPoem link is on the home page.

THE INS AND OUTS OF MEDITATING: There are two approaches to learning how to meditate: you can pay for the instruction, or you can acquire this knowledge for free. There are many websites devoted to meditation, and many of those sites offer free instruction. I initially paid for my meditation instruction. In my case that 60 bucks I laid down for the class "encouraged" me to continue meditating so I wouldn't waste the money I'd spent for instruction. But that was when I was younger, and back then I needed a money incentive to keep my feet to the fire. Since that initial instruction I have taken up a new mantra, quite different from the mantra I was originally given, and I found the mantra on a website that makes it available for nothing.

WHAT'S A MANTRA? A *mantra* is a phrase you say over and over in your mind. You want the phrase to be meaningless because you don't want to cling to it in a meaningful way. Instead you want to recite in your mind, over and over and over, this simple phrase. **You put your attention to the phrase** and nothing else. This helps to give the mind focus. The mantra I use is "maranatha, (m**ah**-r**ah**-n**ah**-th**ah)**, giving each syllable an "ah" sound. Although **we *don't* speak the mantra audibly as we meditate**, say it a few times outloud so you know what it sounds like. I got this mantra from the good people at "The World Community for Christian Meditation" at http://www.wccm.org/, should you want to know more.

HOW TO MEDITATE: So how might we begin to meditate? It's as simple as breathing. First turn off your phone. (A ringing phone will instantly undo your meditative state.) Then find a room or location you feel comfortable in and sit down in a comfortable chair. If at all possible, always meditate in this same place and in this same chair. Don't slump. You don't want to fall asleep. Sit as straight as you can without slouching. (If you are unable to sit, you can also lie down.) For this simple instruction, we will leave the flute out of the process, for now. Begin by sitting quietly for a couple of minutes. Pay attention to your breath as you sit. After a couple of minutes, begin to say your mantra ***in your mind.*** Ma-ra-na-tha, ma-ra-na-tha, ma-ra-na-tha, ma-ra-na-tha, etc., over and over again. Give your total attention to the mantra as you repeat it in your mind. Don't think of anything except the mantra. Pointedly fix your attention on the pronounciation of each syllable as you say the mantra in your mind. When you find your mind drifting away, (and you will), don't be upset with yourself. Simply direct your thinking, once again, to your mantra. Continue to say your mantra for ten to twenty minutes. Even longer, if you like. When the mind drifts away from the mantra, gently bring it back.

After a few minutes you might be ecstatic with your success. Or you might think you are having no success at all. But it doesn't matter how you feel about your session. All you need to do is say the phrase over and over, whether you can stay focused on the mantra or not. Don't worry about the success or failure of your meditation session while you are meditating. And don't worry about it after you meditate, either. Don't wonder if you are going into a state of meditation. Don't try to "go somewhere". The only thing you need to worry about is saying the mantra again and again. This will focus you and shut out distractions so your mind can function fully. And really, that's all there is to it.

THE BREATH AS MANTRA: Another way to meditate is to pay attention to the breath instead of a phrase. This is using your breath as your mantra and as a point of focus. I find this difficult. That's why I use a mantra that can be vocalized. With the breath method the mantra is the breath. But I can't focus on the breath. I prefer to focus on a mantra that's a phrase you can audibly say but don't. I encourage you to experiment with both methods for a few days. But don't wait too long before making your final decision. The power is in repeating the mantra, whether it's word or breath. There is no power in indecision. Decide and then stick with it. By the way, both the breath method and mantra method are thousands of years old, so choosing either puts you in very good company.

Many electronic aids are now available to enhance your meditation sessions. In fact, there's a whole industry that's grown up around meditation. But the core of meditation is saying your mantra, or paying attention to the breath, (if you should choose the breath method). The extraneous stuff is fun to use, but the essence of meditation is the mantra. You don't need anything beyond this simple technique to meditate.

HOW TO MEDITATE WITH THE FLUTE: The Native American flute is an excellent flute to meditate with. It's small and light, but it has a deeper and richer sound than something like the popular standard D pennywhistle. There's nothing wrong with the pennywhistle, but this kind of small-barreled instrument with its high range is better suited to something like energetic Celtic playing or dancing. On the other hand, The Native American flute with its rich, full bodied tone is a contemplative instrument that takes you to a quiet space. To meditate with it is quite simple. To begin, establish yourself in that special place where you meditate, or where you execute your mindful movement routine. If you bike or run, you can meditate with your flute before you walk out the door.

To begin, sit with your flute on your lap. Close your eyes, bow your head, breathe quietly for a minute or two as you establish a certain level of peace, then pick up your flute and softly begin playing. Don't play fast, and don't go for volume. Play slowly and softly. I usually play my flute for a few minutes. Then I lay the flute back on my lap, establish a light grip on it, and then begin silently reciting my mantra. This time period will be my regular mantra meditation session that might last as long as 20 or 30 minutes. But as you meditate, hold the flute. It's comforting. It grounds you as you meditate.

When you finish your meditation session, put the flute back in its regular resting place and either go about your day, slip into your mindfulness routine, or whatever routine you practice on a daily basis. It's as simple as that, but it's a highly effective form of "simple".

I didn't use a flute when I began meditating in 1975. That's because I didn't know how to play the Native American flute. I didn't even own one back then. But once I started using the flute, I found a deeper peace during every meditation session.

-Chapter 3-

Reference

How to Hold the Flute
How to Read Tablature
How to Read Note Duration
How to Add Special Effects

REFERENCE MATERIAL: The section from page 30 to page 54 contains material you will access on a refer-to-it-as-needed basis. You can come back to this reference section when you want to restudy the concepts.

-How to Hold the Flute-

There are two major flute designs. The more popular design features a tapered blowing end (1st photo) where we encircle the end with our lips. We DO NOT use our teeth! That will quickly ruin the flute. The other flute design (2nd photo) is a simple squared off end where we put it up against our lips. We DO NOT encircle the end with our lips. Although the tapered end shown in the first photo is the most popular design, I much prefer the squared-off design you see in the second photo. (The first flute is a cedar flute while the second flute with the squared-off end is made from bamboo.)

-Tonguing Notes-

We can add emphasis to a note by *tonguing* the note. Silently make a 't' sound with your tongue. Now put the flute to your lips, all holes open, and silently make the 't' sound just once as you blow the note. We usually hold the note after we blow it. Notice how the beginning of the note is emphasized with the tonguing action of the silent 't'. This technique, of course, can be used on any note, the note can be held for as long as called for, and tonguing is used more than any other playing technique we might discuss.

-Setting Up the Flute For Best Tone-

If you buy a flute online, it will most likely not be properly set up when you receive it in the mail. The photos above show the setup steps. The flute has two barrel holes at the blowing end as seen in the first photo. The top hole must be covered by the moveable totem, (sometimes called the "block"), as you see in the second photo. The third photo close-up gives you a clearer idea of how close the edge of the totem must be to the edge of the uncovered hole. To fine tune for final tone, lightly tie down the totem so you can still move it. Then slightly change the location of the totem until you get the clearest tone. You don't have to move the totem much to dramatically change the tone, so be very careful. Move, test blow, move, test blow until you're satisfied. Then securely tie down the totem so it can't move. Always check the totem before beginning a new playing session. Even if you have tightly tied down the totem, it's still possible to bump the totem out of alignment. Other popular "fipple" flutes like the penny whistle or the hand crafted recorder for classical music don't have a problem with misalignment. Everything is permanently fixed in place during construction. But the Native American flute is a more elemental instrument. It needs continual care. And that's what makes the Native American flute so much fun!

-Setting Up the PVC WindPoem Flute-

If you prefer an easier flute to setup, consider the WindPoem PVC flute with its unique ring block. The ring is a friction fit on the barrel, and the setup is exactly like the instructions on the previous page, except it's far easier to do. You just slide the ring to the edge of the sound hole, adjusting until you get the best tone.

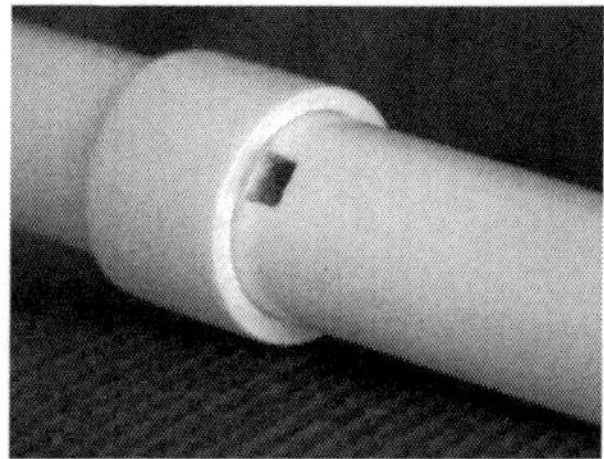

-Generating a Best Tone-

Straight tone, no effect: There are several ways to affect the tone. One way is to smoothly blow without attempting to change the *character* of the tone at all. Just smoothly and steadily blow. This will deliver a very pure tone.

The ***Tremolo:*** The **most important** ***special*** **effect to learn is the** ***tremolo.*** To know what this effect sounds like, think back to when you were a kid, (or you might still be a kid), and you imitated the sound of a car that won't start. That's the physical movement of the abdomen we're looking for. Of course, we make this car-starting sound silently as we blow the note. The slight movement of the abdomen slightly changes the volume, giving the note an etherical sound. All those who play wind instruments use this technique. (Recall the sound of an opera singer.)

TABLATURE OPENS THE DOOR: Some of you might not know how to read music. That's okay. You won't need that knowledge for this book. We will be using a "tablature" notation that makes knowledge of standard music notation unnecessary. The tablature we will use works for any 6-hole Native American flute, regardless of what key the flute might be in.

FLUTE KEYS: As previously discussed, flutes come in various keys. The G flute is higher than the F# flute, an F# is higher than an E, the E is higher than a D, and the D is higher than a C# flute. The G flute is a popular key because it's easy for guitar players to accompany you. But the F# key is also a very popular flute key. The low C# isn't as popular, because it's more difficult for beginning flute players to play well. The barrel has a much greater diameter, and the note holes are larger.

The three flutes I play the most are my F# flute, my E flute, and my low C# flute, all bamboo. I like the sound of a low flute, but I don't use the C# for everything. If you are going to buy just one flute and never another, let that flute be an F#. The tone is brilliant and they are easy to finger.

TABLATURE DESIGNED ESPECIALLY FOR THIS BOOK: Although I use a more sophisticated form of tablature with my PDF *e-book* flute instruction books, (see all my other Native American flute instruction books at FluteFlights.com), those books have a larger page area in comparison to this portable book that's small enough to throw into your gym bag. My purpose with this small book in print is to include many tunes, and that requires a more compact tablature notation to fit in a book of this size. The new **enhanced ASCII tablature** I've devised specifically for this book is the perfect tab form for the type of music we will be exploring. (Wikipedia.org has an excellent article on tablature, including a type of ASCII tablature.)

-TABLATURE-

TABLATURE SHOWS FINGER PLACEMENT: Tablature shows you exactly which holes to cover on the flute barrel to make various notes. The illustration below shows you what's meant.

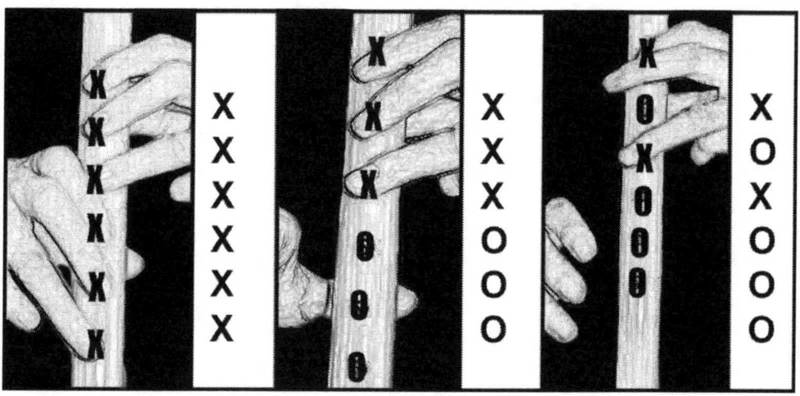

Compare the photos of my fingers to **the simple tablature to the right of each photo**. (The photos show how a right handed player will hold the flute.) We don't need photos or elaborately drawn illustrations. All we need is a column of X's and O's to show how to play the note. Put your fingers where you see Xs and you will play that note. This is a compact way to show where to close each note hole. You don't have to memorize finger placement like you would if we were using standard music notation. Why? Because the complete fingering configuration is in each tabbed note. And that's the real power of tablature; *tablature shows you how to play the tune as you read it!* Tablature is a ***map*** that leads you through the tune.

The Chromatic Scale

THE CHROMATIC SCALE: Like the many-toned music scale of the humpback whale, the music chromatic scale has many tones. (There is also a chromatic scale for *colors,* but that obviously doesn't apply here.) The easiest way to define the *chromatic* scale (in music) is to picture yourself in front of a piano or electronic keyboard where you successively play every white key and every black key as you move up or down the keyboard. If we do this, we find that the interval between any two adjacent notes are a half tone or a *semi tone* apart in pitch. Like the humpback that seems to "sing" every possible note in its own wild compositions, the keyboard also gives us every possible note on the standard musical instrument, whether it be piano or guitar, cello or trumpet.

But we can also play the chromatic scale on any Native American flute. The range of notes won't be as great as on a typical keyboard, but most flutes will give us a minor third above the octave in total pitch range. This means that most flutes give us 15 notes, more than enough notes to play just about any song imaginable. Occasionally a flute will come along that gives us a semi tone above the minor third, but since most don't, we will stay with the 15-tone scale.

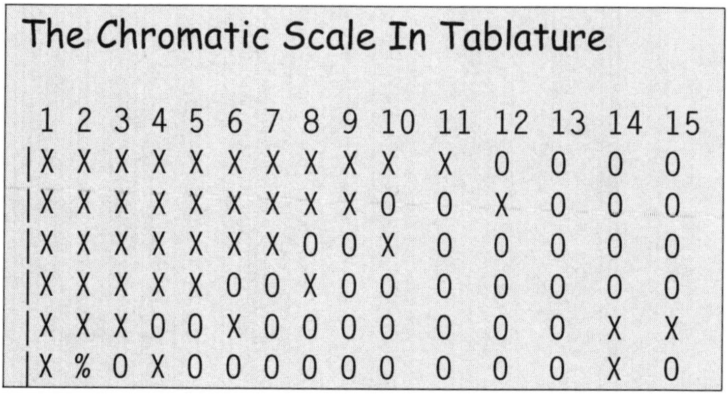

The Chromatic Scale In Tablature

1	2	3	4	5	6	7	8	9	10	11	12	13	14	15
X	X	X	X	X	X	X	X	X	X	X	0	0	0	0
X	X	X	X	X	X	X	X	X	0	0	X	0	0	0
X	X	X	X	X	X	X	0	0	X	0	0	0	0	0
X	X	X	X	X	0	0	X	0	0	0	0	0	0	0
X	X	X	0	0	X	0	0	0	0	0	0	0	X	X
X	%	0	X	0	0	0	0	0	0	0	0	0	X	0

PLAYING THE HALF-HOLE NOTE: Look at the **second column** (second note). Notice the **%** sign at the bottom note hole. The **%** sign indicates that the hole is to be *half* covered. We accomplish this by just touching the rim of the note hole, allowing some, but not all, of the air to escape. If you're careful, you can force **a new note** that's *one whole step*, as we say in the language of music, above the lowest note where all holes are closed.

This added half-hole note greatly increases the melodic possibilities of the flute. Most professional musicians that play the Native American flute use this half-hole note for this very reason.

TECHNICAL *DUST:* Since the first note in the "chromatic" scale is one whole step below the second note, the actual "chromatic" scale begins on the second note, not on the first note. However, since most of the scale is chromatic in nature, (a half-step interval between adjacent notes), I call all 15 notes the "chromatic" scale, out of simple convenience.

THE IMPORTANCE OF SCALES: Do you need to memorize the chromatic scale? No. You don't have to memorize *any* of the scales in this book. I only present them as reference. The tablature for all of the tunes shows you *exactly* how to play each note. Follow the tablature, regardless of flute key, and you'll successfully play the tune.

Pentatonic Scale

WHAT IS THE PENTATONIC SCALE, AND WHY SHOULD WE EVEN CARE ABOUT IT? Simply put, the Pentatonic scale is a group of notes that almost always sounds good regardless of the order you play the notes. (The Pentatonic scale, like all scales, is a subset of the Chromatic scale.) Melodies composed within this scale sound very meditative and mysterious. This is why the Native American flute is a perfect meditative instrument. Melodies are easy to compose, even for beginners, using just the notes from this scale, and evidence of this beautiful scale goes back thousands of years. In the history of music on this planet, the Pentatonic scale is the most basic and was probably the first important scale to be devised. (Deliberately placed musical intervals have been found on a 30,000-year-old flute made from a vulture wing bone.)

You've heard the blues. The roots of the blues is in this simple 5-note scale. (That's why I put that image of a female blues guitar player in the header.) You've heard jazz. The roots of jazz is in the Pentatonic scale. You've heard gospel music. You've heard folk music. And classical music. All these musical genres, and more, use melodies composed from the Pentatonic scale.

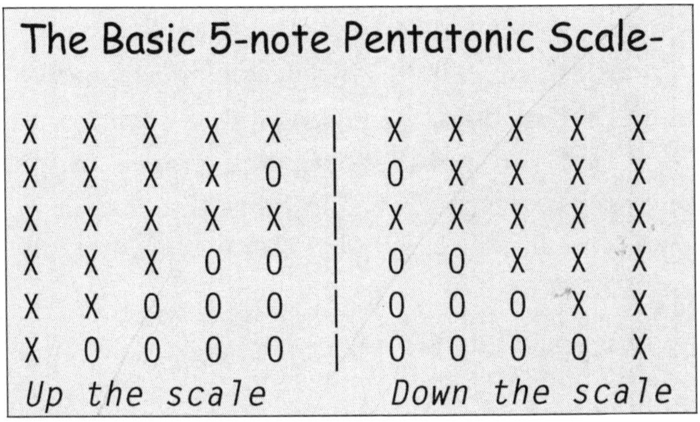

The Basic 5-note Pentatonic Scale-

```
X  X  X  X  X  |  X  X  X  X  X
X  X  X  X  0  |  0  X  X  X  X
X  X  X  X  X  |  X  X  X  X  X
X  X  X  0  0  |  0  0  X  X  X
X  X  0  0  0  |  0  0  0  X  X
X  0  0  0  0  |  0  0  0  0  X
Up the scale      Down the scale
```

The TAB shows closed holes, X, and open holes, O. ***Each column** of six characters is one note.* Close the holes where you see an X, then *blow **gently** to get the lower notes*, and more briskly as you play the higher notes. The lowest note on your flute is played with all holes closed. So the first column in the TAB is the lowest note any Native American flute can produce. But be careful when playing this lowest note: If you blow too hard, you'll get squawks. With most flutes it takes just a *gentle* breath to get that lowest note. Try playing this scale from lower to higher. Remember to blow easy on the lower notes and harder on the higher notes. Notice that the scale goes up in pitch in the first section and down in pitch in the second section.

SECTIONING OFF INTO MEASURES: Each section in a tablature is called a "measure". There are two measures in the Pentatonic scale tablature above, and that vertical bar in the tablature marks it off into two measures. In tunes with specific rhythms, each measure has the same number of beats. The tune might have 4 beats per measure. Some songs have 3 beats per measure. We can also play tunes at 6 beats per measure, (6 b/m), 7 b/m, 5 b/m, etc. (We will only be concerned with 4 b/m and 3 b/m in this book.)

CAN WE ADD NOTES TO THE PENTATONIC SCALE? There are just five notes in the Pentatonic scale, and these five notes give us many melody possibilities. But we can extend the scale dramatically, while still maintaining the *spirit* of the original scale. We extend the **range** of the scale by adding the **octave note** and **two notes above** the octave. Adding these three new notes extends the scale from the original five notes to eight notes.

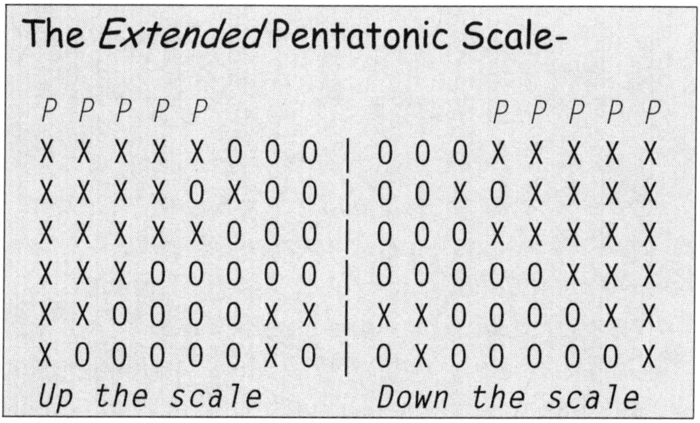

The *Extended* Pentatonic Scale-

```
P P P P P                    P P P P P
X X X X X 0 0 0 | 0 0 0 X X X X X
X X X X 0 X 0 0 | 0 0 X 0 X X X X
X X X X X 0 0 0 | 0 0 0 X X X X X
X X X 0 0 0 0 0 | 0 0 0 0 0 X X X
X X 0 0 0 0 X X | X X 0 0 0 0 X X
X 0 0 0 0 0 X 0 | 0 X 0 0 0 0 0 X
Up the scale      Down the scale
```

NOTE: The extended Pentatonic scale, as tabbed above, now has a total of eight notes rather than just five notes. Notice that the original Pentatonic scale is embedded in the extended scale and is made up of those notes below those mysterious little P's I've put along the top of the tablature. Those notes *not under* a *P* are notes that *extend* the basic Pentatonic scale, but are not part of the original scale. Try playing this extended scale on your flute. When you play this tablature, you'll notice that the first half of the tablature, or TAB, (from now on we will often substitute the word "TAB" for "tablature"), goes up the scale, while the second section goes down the scale. You will have to blow harder on each note as you go up the scale, with the highest note requiring the most blowing power. Listen carefully as you progress up the scale. *Each note should sound a bit higher than the previous note.*

TABLATURE IS A *RELATIVE* NOTATION: The huge advantage to tablature is that it's a *relative* notation. I've spoken of this previously, but it's an important concept that bears repeating. Since each tabbed note shows you which holes to cover to make a particular note, everything will always sound correct, *relatively.* Using just one tablature, if you play something like "Mary Had a Little Lamb" on a flute that's built in the key of *G*, and then play the same tune, using that same tablature, on a flute that's built in the lower key of *C#*, you will recognize the tune on both flutes, but the melody on the *G* flute will sound higher than that same melody played on the low *C#* flute, even though you've used the same tablature to play both. This demonstrates the fact that the tablature is universally applicable to any 6-hole Native American flute, *regardless of the key of the flute.*

Tablature was developed hundreds of years ago, and it made possible for those with little or no formal training in the standard western music notation to play an instrument in a comprehensive way. One might think tablature was developed for amateur musicians of the time, but tablature was also embraced by the professional musician. Tablature was especially popular during the Renaissance and Baroque eras, and tablature was written for many types of instruments including the organ, fretted instruments like the lute, the "vihuela", (a guitar-like instrument), the ocarina, the harp, etc. And in the present day we still use tablature for all types of popular instruments, including the guitar and banjo. Tablature is especially useful when writing music for "folk" instruments.

DURATION NUMBERS: Most of the melodies we are familiar with use notes of varying durations. So we will need a way to indicate the amount of time (duration) each note should be held. There are several ways to indicate note duration in tablature. In this book we will use simple numbers and symbols below the notes. In regard to the illustrations to follow, since we are only interested in studying the *duration* of different notes, we aren't interested in the note itself. To simplify, then, the lowest note played with all holes closed will be our "dummy" note because we needn't concern ourselves with the actual note. We will only pay attention to the various duration number combinations written below each note.

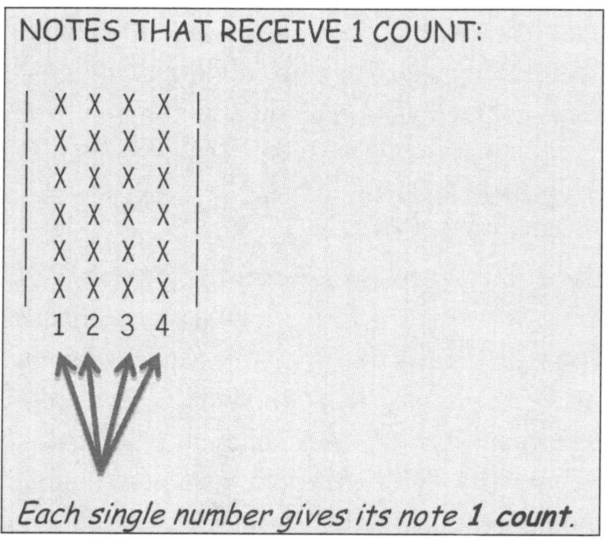

*Each single number gives its note **1 count**.*

When we see a single number below a note, it means the note gets just 1 count. The *empirical* amount, how big or small the number is, (2, 3, whatever), is irrevelant to the *duration.* This number only shows us where we are in the measure as we play through it. Note #1 gets 1 count, and note #3 gets 1 count.

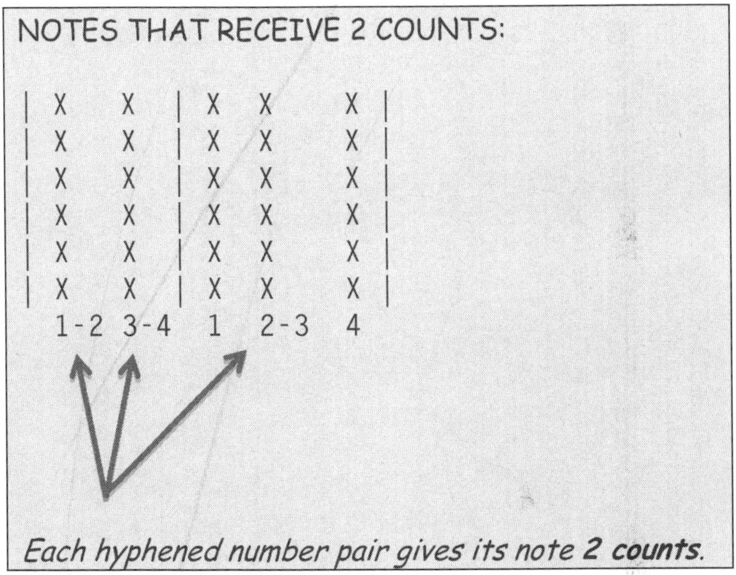

NOTES THAT RECEIVE 2 COUNTS:

```
| X   X  | X  X    X |
| X   X  | X  X    X |
| X   X  | X  X    X |
| X   X  | X  X    X |
| X   X  | X  X    X |
| X   X  | X  X    X |
  1-2 3-4  1  2-3  4
```

*Each hyphened number pair gives its note **2 counts**.*

When we play a tune, it's helpful with unfamiliar melodies to silently and *evenly* count off the duration numbers as we play through the tune. Since it takes twice as long to count "1, 2" than it does to count just "1", or just "2", the note will be held through two counts. **Two duration numbers connected with a hyphen gives a single note a duration of two counts.**

NOTES THAT RECEIVE 3 COUNTS:
Play 3 times

```
| X       X | X X      |
| X       X | X X      |
| X       X | X X      |
| X       X | X X      |
| X       X | X X      |
| X       X | X X      |
  1-2-3   4   1 2-3-4
```

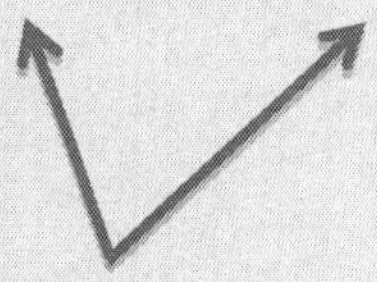

*Each hyphened number triple gives its note **3 counts**.*

If we evenly count "1, 2, 3", doing this will take three times longer than counting just "1", or just "2", or just "3". **Three duration numbers connected with hyphens gives a single note a duration of three counts.**

NOTES THAT ARE TIED INTO THE NEXT MEASURE: **When note clusters are connected *across measures* with the '~' character, the note is first blown, then held to the end of the measure, then held into the next measure for the number of counts indicated by the duration numbers below the note.**

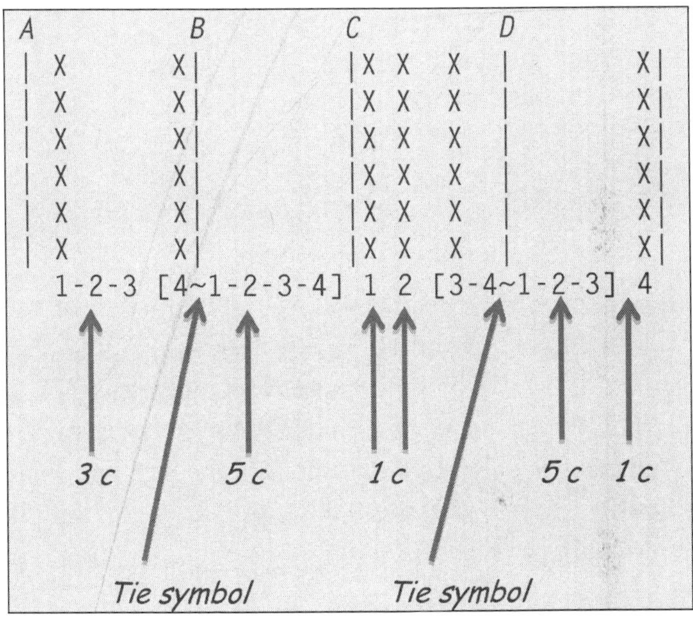

Notice that even though there is no note in measure B, the note is there because it was blown and held for 1 count in the previous measure, A, then held for 4 counts into the next "empty" measure B because of the '~' character connecting duration numbers across measures. The same is true for measures C and D. The last note in measure C is blown and held for 2 counts, and then 3 counts into measure D. The tip-off is the ~ tie symbol connecting the duration numbers. (The [ ] symbols for clarification are used only for this example, but not ordinarily used.)

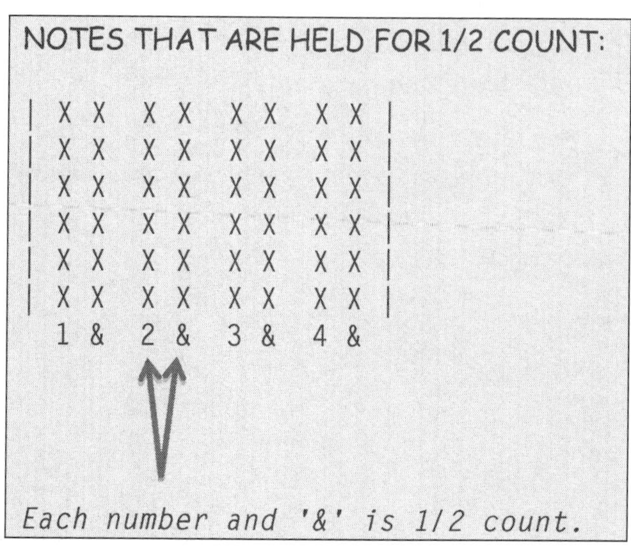

The & character is used to show notes that receive a half count. When this & character *follows* a number, the note with the number, as well as the note with the & character, gets a half count. The lyrics to the familiar tune, "Skip to My Lou", demonstrates this concept. If you simply say the lyrics out loud, you will understand the values of the duration numbers below each word or syllable.

I've got a red bird a blue bird'll do....
1 2 & 3 4 & 1 2 & 3-4

I've got a red bird a blue bird'll do....
1 2 & 3 4 & 1 2 & 3-4

I've got a red bird a blue bird'll do....
1 2 & 3 4 & 1 2 & 3-4

Skip to my Lou, my dar......lin'
1 2 & 3 4 1-2 3-4

```
PICKUP NOTES:

|         X|X X X X |
|         X|X X X X |
|         X|X X X X |
|         X|X X X X |
|         X|X X X X |
|         X|X X X X |
   1 2 3 4 1 2 3 4
```

In the example above, the first three *gray* duration numbers are *silently* counted but not blown because no notes are with the beat numbers. The actual blown "pickup note" is the 4th note in this first measure.

The concept of the **pickup note** can be clarified with the familiar lyrics of "Happy Birthday". We don't begin singing until after we have silently counted off the first 2 beats in gray. The actual pickup note begins with the syllable "HAP py". in this first measure. If you simply say the lyrics out loud, you will understand the duration numbers below each word or syllable.

```
    Hap-py Birth-day to you  Hap-py
1 2  3  &    1    2  3  1-2   3  &

Birth-day to you  Hap-py
  1    2   3  1-2   3  &

Birth-day dear Grand-ma..........Hap-py
  1    2    3     1    2           3  &

Birth-day to you
  1    2   3  1-2
```

It Ain't Gonna Rain No More No More!

Here's one more example to help you match the actual rhythm of a tune with its duration numbers. This is a fun American folk tune my grandma used to sing to me. Even if you aren't familiar with the melody, just reciting the words out loud will make clear the meaning of the duration numbers below the words and syllables. Notice the three pickup notes. The lyrics don't begin until *after* these numbers are silently counted.

It ain't gon-na rain no more no more, it
1 2 3 4 1 2 & 3 4 1 2 3 4

Ain't gon-na rain no more........
1 2 & 3 4 1-2-3-4

How in the dic-kens can I wa-ter my chic-kens if it
1 2 & 3 & 4 & 1 & 2 3 & 4 &

Ain't gon-na rain no more........
1 2 & 3 4 1-2-3

-Adding Ornamentation-

THE TRILL: It's fun to add flair and panache to our playing. We do this in a number of ways, but we are never required to use these techniques. In fact, some flute players don't use fancy techniques at all. *Shakuhachi* flute players, *(traditional end-blown Japanese bamboo flute),* who play meditatively seldom use any effects. Nevertheless, these techniques are still interesting and fun to experiment with.

The Trill (warble) Effect:

Trl	Trl	Trl	Trl	Trl
X X	X X	X X	0 0	X X
X X	X X	*x o*	*x o*	X X
X X	X X	X X	0 0	X X
X X	*x o*	0 0	0 0	*x o*
X X	0 0	0 0	0 0	*x o*
x o	0 0	0 0	0 0	0 0

The TRILL effect sounds like a warbling bird. Rapidly open and close *only* the hole(s) indicated by the italicized note hole(s) in the tablature *while holding everything else in place.* **Each pair of notes is really just one note**, but we alter the note by opening and closing only those particular holes that are indicated by *lowercase* italics. When we open and close these *italicized* note holes quickly, the effect sounds quite beautiful. Looking at the example above, we see the trill applied to notes as they go up the scale. There are other places where we can apply the trill effect, and you'll discover those the more you become familiar with your flute.

Realize that it requires two notes to make a trilled note. With the note hole to be trilled closed, while blowing the note, lift the finger, or fingers, off to make the second note of the pair, then put the finger(s) back, then lift, then put back. This opening and closing is done rapidly and as many times as you like before ending back on the first note. You can also do this in reverse with the note hole to be trilled open, and the second note hole to be trilled closed. The rapid opening and closing of a note hole is done while the note is sounding.

Notice the 4th note in this TAB. The alternate opening and closing of a note hole takes place on the 2nd hole from the top, but there are closed note holes *surrounding* the trilled note hole. Another note to examine is the 6th trilled note. In the 6th note we open and close **two notes holes at once** rather than just one note hole. Although this is an impressive technique, it will take almost no time to master.

THE RASPBERRY: Another way to affect the tone is to induce a *raspberry* effect. This is done by allowing the tip of the tongue to rapidly flutter as you blow. It's a novel effect we can get away with once in awhile, but we don't want to use it very often. The purpose of the raspberry is to add novel emphasis to a note or passage. The symbol, **Rrr**... above a note will show you which notes to apply this effect to.

THE SLIDE: The slide is an effect that smoothly raises the pitch or lowers the pitch of a note. It's a pretty effect and is done in various ways, but on the flute it is executed by sliding the fingers ***onto*** a note hole to (C)lose it, or ***off*** a note hole to (O)pen it.

If you are sliding onto a note hole, make sure your finger is anchored on the barrel next to a hole, and then **slowly** slide your finger over the ***italicized*** note hole until it's closed. In most fingering configurations you will hear the *pitch gradually go lower.* (Think of how a trombone sounds when you slowly pull out the slide.)

If you want to *raise the pitch,* you slowly slide the finger off the ***italicized*** note hole until it's completely open. The tablature will show you which notes you can do this to and which note holes to slide onto and off of.

The two slide symbols are these:

>To raise the pitch , slide (o)pen a lower hole: S-O

> To lower the pitch , slide (c)losed a lower hole: S-C

S-O	S-O	S-O	S-C	S-C	S-C
X X	X X	X X	X X	X X	X X
X X	X X	X X	X X	X X	X X
X X	X X	X X	X X	X X	X X
X X	X X	*x o*	*o x*	X X	X X
X X	*x o*	0 0	0 0	*o x*	X X
x o	0 0	0 0	0 0	0 0	*o x*

We can also slide onto and off of two or three note holes at a time.

THE ***HOLD*** SYMBOL: We know that melodies vary greatly. This is *usually* accomplished by giving the melody notes different time durations. Some notes are held for one count, some for two counts, some for a half count, some notes are held into the next measure, etc. (Recall that tablature symbols for note duration values was covered in the reference section, pages 41 - 47.) But there is another style of playing that's quite different from the kind of music we usually hear. The main tablature symbol for this type of playing is the HOLD symbol. Duration numbers for various notes are used with those tunes that have a strict beat. Although we will explore this type of playing in depth in this book, we will also thoroughly explore "extemporaneous" or "free-style" playing where a tune does not have a strict rhythm. Stepping away from a firm beat allows us to express ourselves in a much freer way. You can't dance to this kind of music—at least not in the sense we think of dancing—but we can find new spiritual spaces within us when we play extemporaneously. So the problem for an author like myself is to write out an extemporaneous tune, in tablature form, that isn't really extemporaneous since you're not coming up with the tune from your own imagination, but *sounds* extemporaneous as you play my tablatures. I solved this problem with the "HOLD" symbol. You will understand the reason for this symbol when you encounter the extemporaneous collection of tunes in the last part of this book. But for future reference, note the following—

The HOLD symbol from shortest to longest:

hold   hold... HOLD...   HOLD......   HOLD.........

THE BARK: This effect is most commonly performed on the Native American flute. To make this effect, blow a note, hold it for as long as you like, and then quickly lift your fingers off some note holes to make a new note, **while at the same time blowing with an explosive burst of air**, thus ending the note abruptly. This gives a woofing or barking sound.

There are two steps to the bark. The first note is blown and held, then the second note is played by quickly lifting fingers to match the second note configuration, exhaling in a huff to make it bark. The notes with an (*) are those notes where you quickly lift your fingers to make the bark. The example below shows you some good note pairs to make a good bark. (The extended hyphens are used to show a pause or long note.)

HOLD *	HOLD *	HOLD *
X----x	X----x	X----0
X----0	X----x	X----x
X----x	X----x	X----0
X----0	X----0	0----0
X----0	X----0	0----0
X----0	X----0	0----0

SHARPLY TONGUING NOTES FOR ADDED EMPHASIS: Sometimes to add extra emphasis to a **group of notes** we *sharply* tongue these notes rather than execute the explosive burst of air we play on the asterisk (*) to make a bark. This sharply tongued note adds some serious emphasis in those places where the gently tongued note, that technique we might use in ordinary playing, isn't enough. The symbol for a sharply tongued note is an italized capital *'T'*.

T	*T*	*T*	*T*	*T*	*T*	*T*	*T*	HOLD......	*
X	X	X	X	X	X	X	X	X-------	X
X	X	X	X	X	X	X	X	X-------	0
X	X	X	X	X	X	X	X	X-------	X
X	0	X	X	X	X	X	X	X-------	0
X	0	0	X	X	X	0	X	X-------	0
X	0	0	0	X	0	0	0	X-------	0

Notice in the example above that the first eight notes are sharply tongued, while the 7th note is blown, held, and then changed to an explosively barked new note on the last note (under the asterisk). These sharply tongued notes can be very effective in those tunes where we want to tell a story. The more variety you command, the more techniques you know, the more powerfully you can tell your story to yourself and to others.

THE GRACE NOTE: A beautiful ornament to a melody is accomplished by *briefly* blowing a note just an *instant* before you play the main melody note. It will take just a bit of practice to make this effect sound good. The ^ symbol above a note means you play this note just long enough to register on the consciousness before moving on to the actual melody note. The grace note is a decorative flourish that sounds pretty if not overdone. (Notice that the note holes that change in each note pair is in italics.)

Try playing the grace note examples below.

^		^		^	^		^	^	^	^	^
X	X	X	X	*o*	*x*	X	*o*	*x*	X	X	X
X	X	*o*	*x*	*o*	*x*	X	*o*	*x*	X	X	X
X	X	X	X	X	X	X	X	X	X	X	X
X	X	0	0	0	0	*x*	0	0	*x*	X	X
X	X	0	0	0	0	0	0	0	0	*x*	X
o	*x*	0	0	0	0	0	0	0	0	0	*x*

The first and second examples consist of the grace note, followed by the main melody note, which should be held for whatever duration the TAB calls for. The third example has two grace notes, followed by a longer held main note. Example #4 is 5 grace notes. Notice the end note is not a regular note like the other three examples. These five notes as grace notes make a dazzling ending to a tune. You can easily play a spectacular run of notes using the grace note technique. (You can also see me demonstrate all these effects in the video, NAFluteEffects.mp4 that's available on the download page.)

The grace note is the exact opposite of the bark. The grace note is a very quick note that comes *before* the main melody note. The bark is a very short note that comes *after* the main melody note.

-Chapter 4-

Long Note Chants
Baby Chants

BUILDING BLOCKS: Whenever we are ready to learn something new, all too often we impatiently want to learn it all at once. So we jump in, feet first, become frustrated because we didn't take it step-by-step, and end up learning nothing at all. If you are currently practicing yoga, you know that trying poses that are well beyond your skill level will end up hurting you, both physically and emotionally. And so, the wise student will listen to the teacher and take things at a safe and productive speed, eventually working up to the more complex poses. So as you begin your exploration of the Native American flute, think of me as your teacher of this beautiful instrument. I have given hundreds, maybe thousands, (I've truly lost count), of music lessons over the years, and I learned two very important things during this time. First, I learned there are no shortcuts to learning something well. (I highly doubt you one day simply slipped into the Eagle pose or the Crane pose or bicycled 10 miles without gradually working up to it.) Second, from the positive feedback of my students I learned to make the music I taught them easy, interesting, and fun with even the beginning tunes. The secret was to write my own material so I had control over whether the material was interesting and fun, or difficult and boring. I have made all of the material in this book interesting and fun. Even the very first chants are meditative, as well as fun to play. The secret is to play something simple really well.

BLOWING A BEAUTIFUL NOTE: After you have adjusted the block for best tone, (page 31), close all note holes. If you are right handed, your 1st, 2nd, and 3rd fingers of the right hand should cover the bottom three holes. These are the holes at the bottom of the flute when you hold it in the playing position, (like a clarinet). Cover the top three holes with your 1st, 2nd, and 3rd fingers of the left hand. (Photos for hand placement is on page 34.) If you are left-handed, then switch hand positions. Now, with all six holes closed, blow very gently. If you get squawks, you are blowing too hard, or you don't have one or more of the holes sealed, or both. Adjust your fingers, blow more gently and try again. You should get a low, beautiful tone. Once you achieve this, practice blowing this lowest note until it becomes easy for you. As you blow the note, close your eyes and focus on the sound. Become lost in the sound. Picture yourself as a majestic humpback whale, singing across the ocean with your flute. When you are satisfied with your effort, lift just your 3rd finger off the bottom hole. Then try to blow this new note. Use the Pentatonic scale chart to blow each note clearly as you slowly but surely work your way up the scale. Once again, close your eyes and focus on each note. Try to hold each note as long as you can. Once you think you've made progress with this, play the second measure of the Pentatonic scale and slowly work your way back down. You can meditate with just these long notes. The tunes you play don't have to be complex to be effective. A good warm-up is to slowly play up the scale and then back down the scale before going on to more complex tunes. So let's review the Pentatonic scale, the most basic scale "native" to the Native American flute.

Pentatonic Scale-

X	X	X	X	X	|	X	X	X	X	X
X	X	X	X	0	|	0	X	X	X	X
X	X	X	X	X	|	X	X	X	X	X
X	X	X	0	0	|	0	0	X	X	X
X	X	0	0	0	|	0	0	0	X	X
X	0	0	0	0	|	0	0	0	0	X
Up->						*Down->*				

TWO DISTINCT SONG STYLES: The kind of music most of us consider familiar is music with an evenly metered rhythm. Pick any tune you might know, sing it or listen to it, and you instinctively know the tune has a rhythm you can tap your foot to. Rap artists rap with a rhythmic background, rock and country artists play with a rhythmic beat, and this beat is almost always 4b/m. Four beats per measure is the most common meter for popular music. But sing the song, "Happy Birthday", and you will sing it at 3 b/m. Some years back the Dave Brubeck Quartet, a popular jazz quartet, released a tune called "Take 5", where the rhythm was 5 b/m. This was a brand new rhythm to we common folk, and although it took us all a while to learn to hum the tune in the correct rhythm, it eventually seemed like we had been humming and playing this no longer strange rhythm all our lives. Traditional Greek music, music that's been around for hundreds of years, often uses 7 b/m. Classical compositions as well as sophisticated rock groups like to use a combination of rhythms in just one tune. They will play a couple of phrases at 5 b/m, then play a couple of phrases at 7 b/m, then maybe a few phrases at 12 b/m. We won't be getting this involved with strange rhythms, but knowing that most tunes are usually composed and performed with a steady beat helps us become comfortable with the flute.

But there is another style of playing. This style has no discernable steady rhythm. Although I call this style the "Extemporaneous Style" or "free-style", the word *extemporaneous* meaning "spontaneous" or "adlibbed", (composing tunes from our imagination and on the fly), we can also *write down* in tablature form extemporaneous tunes played in a spontaneous way. In this book we will study this style, because playing this way is meditative in its own special way. I will give you the notes in the tablature for extemporaneous tunes, along with some hints as to when to hold some notes. But the final performance will be up to you.

HOW WE APPROACH THESE TWO STYLES IN THIS BOOK: As previously noted, those tunes played with a steady rhythm are the most familiar to us. The easiest, and by far the most pleasant way to learn to play the flute is by studying music in this form. We leave it to the latter part of the book, after you are more experienced, to explore extemporaneous tunes.

So let's begin our studies with those tunes that have a definite rhythm. **Those *numbers you will see below each note* in a TAB is your guide to proper note duration.** (Duration and what the numbers mean was explained in detail on pages 41 - 47 of the reference section.) So let's begin our studies of note duration at the simplest level.

-Long Note Meditations-

When we meditate, *simplicity* is the key. That mantra we place our focus on should be simple and clean. When we use our flute for meditation, we want what we play to be simple and free flowing. It can have a level of complexity that engages us, but a simple note can be equally engaging. So let's begin our studies with simple chants that won't frustrate us.

```
Breath Meditation #1:

A         B
|X        |        ||
|X        |        ||
|X        |        ||
|X        |        ||
|X        |        ||
|X        |        ||
 1-2-3-4~1-2-3-4
```

In this simple chant all holes are closed. This gives us the lowest possible note on the flute. This note requires almost no breath, because if you blow even a little bit too hard, you will get squawks. To blow this note successfully, make sure all holes are tightly closed. Then *blow with a force of a gentle exhale.* Doing this yields a beautiful note that sails smoothly from the barrel. **Notice the letters A and B at the top of the TAB. These are labels for the measures** so I can refer you to specific places in the TAB. Notice the numbers below the TAB. All those numbers, in this particular chant, are connected in duration with characters (-) and (~), giving the one note in this TAB a total duration of 8 counts. As soon as you blow the note, begin counting silently and evenly as you continue to blow the note through 8 counts.

Breath Meditation #2:

```
A          B          C          D
|X         |X         |X         |         ||
|X         |X         |X         |         ||
|X         |X         |X         |         ||
|X         |X         |X         |         ||
|X         |X         |X         |         ||
|X         |0         |X         |         ||
 1-2-3-4   1-2-3-4   1-2-3-4~1-2-3-4
```

This meditation has three notes. Begin with all holes closed, the lowest note on your flute. Blow and hold for 4 even counts, (1-2-3-4), through measure A. In measure B, open the bottom hole, blow and hold for 4 even counts, (1-2-3-4), through measure B. Then close the bottom hole in measure C and blow and hold for 8 even counts, (1-2-3-4~1-2-3-4), through measures C and D. Notice the ~ character between measures C and D which combines those duration values in measure C to those in measure D. All duration numbers must be given an equal value of 1 count. Counting evenly gives the tune a rhythmic structure.

Breath Meditation #3:

```
A          B          C          D
|X    X    |X    X    |X         |         ||
|X    X    |X    X    |X         |         ||
|X    X    |X    X    |X         |         ||
|X    X    |X    X    |X         |         ||
|X    X    |0    X    |X         |         ||
|X    0    |0    0    |X         |         ||
 1-2  3-4  1-2  3-4  1-2-3-4~1-2-3-4
```

Each of the five notes in the TAB on the previous page, Breath Meditation #3, is blown and held for the time indicated by the duration numbers connected to each note. The first note in measure A is blown and held through 2 counts, (1-2). The second note in measure A is blown and held through 2 counts, (3-4). The first note in measure B is blown and held for 2 counts, (1-2), while the second note in measure B is blown and held for 2 counts, (3-4). The first and only note in measure C is blown and held for 4 counts, (1-2-3-4), and the (~) character tells us to hold it through another 4 counts in measure D, (1-2-3-4~1-2-3-4), for 8 counts.

You should try composing some of your own easy chants. What's most important is to silently and evenly count to yourself in **groups of four**. This gives the chant a structured feel. And even though we will dispense with the rhythmic feel of a chant when we study the free-style chant later on in this book, you will never be comfortable with the free-style until you first master the structured, rhythmic style we are already so familiar with.

As you can imagine, our chants will become somewhat more complex as we move through this book. Added complexity will not destroy the meditative quality if we learn to play through the complexity with ease. To help bring us up to speed, we will consider a couple of familiar tunes. A very familiar tune can enlighten us in various ways. It has been my experience that students will almost immediately understand the meaning of duration values when they see them used in a familiar tune. Play the TAB that follows, but pay special attention to the duration numbers below each note, even though you already know the correct way to play this tune. (Some of the tunes in this book will occasionally use notes beyond the extended Pentatonic scale. Don't let this concern you. The finger placement information is in each note, so you won't have to memorize anything. Just follow the TAB.)

Mary Had a Little Lamb: A - H.

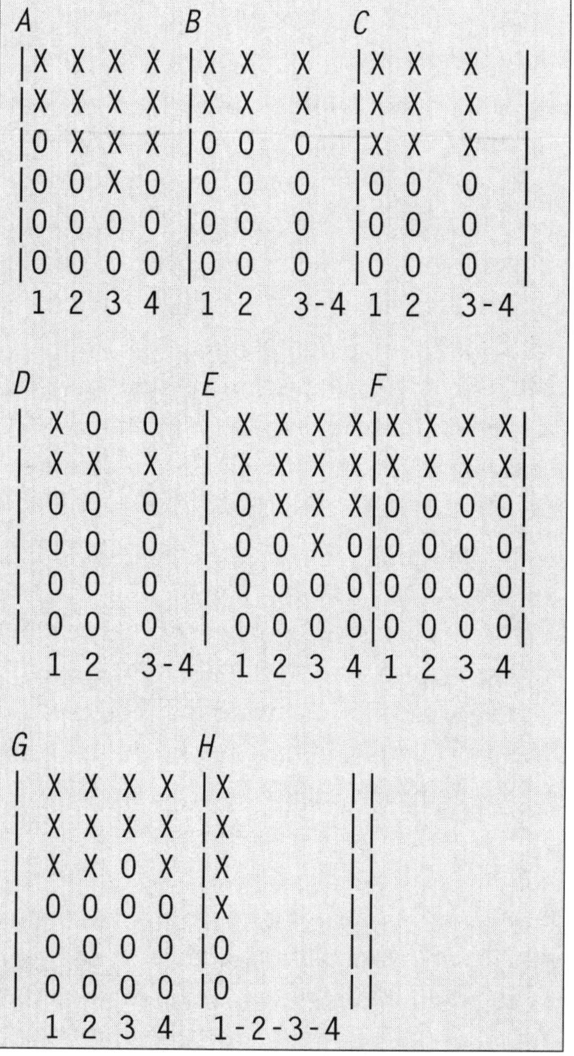

```
A           B           C
|X X X X |X X   X   |X X   X   |
|X X X X |X X   X   |X X   X   |
|0 X X X |0 0   0   |X X   X   |
|0 0 X 0 |0 0   0   |0 0   0   |
|0 0 0 0 |0 0   0   |0 0   0   |
|0 0 0 0 |0 0   0   |0 0   0   |
 1 2 3 4  1 2   3-4  1 2   3-4

D           E         F
| X 0   0   | X X X X|X X X X|
| X X   X   | X X X X|X X X X|
| 0 0   0   | 0 X X X|0 0 0 0|
| 0 0   0   | 0 0 X 0|0 0 0 0|
| 0 0   0   | 0 0 0 0|0 0 0 0|
| 0 0   0   | 0 0 0 0|0 0 0 0|
  1 2   3-4   1 2 3 4 1 2 3 4

G         H
| X X X X |X       ||
| X X X X |X       ||
| X X 0 X |X       ||
| 0 0 0 0 |X       ||
| 0 0 0 0 |0       ||
| 0 0 0 0 |0       ||
  1 2 3 4  1-2-3-4
```

So "Mary Had a Little Lamb" isn't at the top of your greatest hits list? That's okay. It's not at the top of mine, either. But this familiar tune immediately makes clear notes of more than 1 count, those notes connected with hyphens. Notice that the last note in measure B has 3-4 under it. Counting 3-4 with a hyphen connecting the numbers means this note is held through 2 counts. Notice that the last notes (third notes) in measures C and D also have a 3-4 under it. It means the note is held through 2 counts. The last measure, measure H, has just one note, but the 1-2-3-4 underneath means the note is held through 4 counts. (The double bar at the end of the TAB is used to show that it's the end of the tune.) **The simple *hyphen* ties beats together so we can represent notes with a duration longer than one count.** By the way, even though this tune might not be in your top ten of favorite hits, playing it for your kids or grand kids will put YOU on the top of THEIR hits list. ☺

PLAYING ORDER: Notice that the playing instructions after the TAB title tell you to play measures A through H. This is the simplest playing order of a tune. The playing order in some tunes won't be obvious, and sometimes it will be complex. Get into the habit of checking the playing order before starting a tune. It will always be there after the TAB title.

To learn even more about note duration, let's explore the various aspects of it with some practice chants. We will call these introductory chants "baby chants".

Every note in Baby Chant #1 has a 1 count value for each note. We know this because a single number, 1, 2, 3, or 4, with nothing else connected to the numbers, means the note gets one count. All notes in this chant have the same duration of 1 beat, or count. ***Tongue* each note as you play to add emphasis to each note.** (Refer to page 30 to refresh your memory on how to tongue a note.)

Baby Chant #1: Play A - D

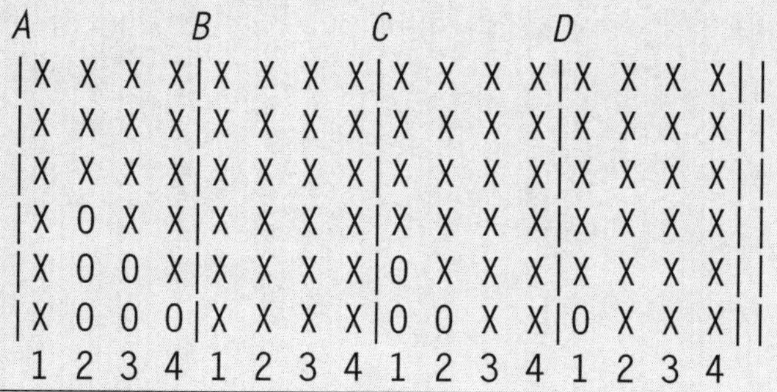

```
A          B          C          D
|X X X X|X X X X|X X X X|X X X X||
|X X X X|X X X X|X X X X|X X X X||
|X X X X|X X X X|X X X X|X X X X||
|X 0 X X|X X X X|X X X X|X X X X||
|X 0 0 X|X X X X|0 X X X|X X X X||
|X 0 0 0|X X X X|0 0 X X|0 X X X||
 1 2 3 4 1 2 3 4 1 2 3 4 1 2 3 4
```

Notice the playing instructions after the title. It tells us to play measures A through D, (A - D). You can repeat this as many times as you wish. Playing a chant over and over is like repeating a mantra; it can put you into a meditative state.

Each letter, A - D, identifies its measure, and this makes it easy to refer you to specific places in a tablature.

DURATION VARIETY ADDS POWER, (A REVIEW): Note duration has been thoroughly covered in the reference material, pages 41-47, but if you didn't read it, the following paragraph will explain it again.

DURATION REVISITED: Although we can play tunes where every note is played for just 1 count, music would be quite boring without some variety. It would be equivalent to playing cards where each and every card was the Jack of Diamonds! Variety adds power, color, and interest. We accomplish this by assigning different durations to notes. Sometimes we do this by lengthening the amount of time a note is held. We can indicate this in music and tablature a number of different ways. In the tablature in this book we are keeping it simple. A note with just a 1, 2, 3, or 4 under it is played for just 1 count. But a note with a 1-2, 2-3, or 3-4 under it is blown and held for two counts. A note with a 1-2-3 or 2-3-4 under it gets three counts. A note with a 1-2-3-4 under it gets four counts. As already illustrated in the reference material, pages 41 through 47, it can get a bit more complex than this. But I will lead you through the more complex duration values as they come up in the various tablatures, (tunes), I've written for you.

Let's rewrite Baby Chant #1 so some of the notes are held for more than one count.

Baby Chant #2: Play A - D.

```
A        B          C         D
|X    X X|X X X X|X     X X|X X X X||
|X    X X|X X X X|X     X X|X X X X||
|X    X X|X X X X|X     X X|X X X X||
|X    0 X|X X X X|X     X X|X X X X||
|X    0 X|X X X X|0     X X|X X X X||
|X    0 0|X X X X|0     0 X|0 X X X||
 1-2  3 4 1 2 3 4 1-2   3 4 1 2 3 4
```

Notice that there are only three notes in measure *A* and only three notes in measure *C*. But there are a full four beats in each measure because the first note is held for 2 counts.

Before playing, if we first say the numbers out loud, we can hear how the rhythm should be. **Speak softly the number that comes after a hyphen**. Like this—

A *B*
One two three four One two three four
2 counts

C *D*
One two three four One two three four
2 counts

I will count off the rhythm in some of the tunes (in the free download audio files) in just this way. If you are having trouble establishing a correct rhythm, refer to these audio files before continuing.

BABY CHANT #3: Play straight through, A - D.

```
A            B           C           D
|X          X|X X       |X X X      |X X X   ||
|X          X|X X       |X X X      |X X X   ||
|X          X|X X       |X X X      |X X X   ||
|X          0|X X       |X X X      |X X X   ||
|X          0|X X       |0 X X      |X X X   ||
|X          0|0 X       |0 0 X      |0 X X   ||
 1-2-3      4 1 2-3-4    1 2 3-4     1 2 3-4
```

4 COUNTS PER MEASURE: Measure A has just two notes, but there are 4 beats. The first note is held for three counts, and the second note gets 1 count. 3 + 1 = 4 counts for that measure. In measure B the first note gets one count, the second note gets three counts. 1 + 3 = 4 counts for that measure. In measure C the first note gets 1 count, the second note gets 1 count, the third note gets 2 counts. 1 + 1 + 2 = 4 counts for that measure. Measure D plays just like measure C and has 4 counts for that measure.

Sometimes we hold notes into the next measure. To indicate where this occurs we use a **~** symbol. Here's an easy illustration of what we mean—

```
        Baby Chant #4: A - D
A          B          C          D
|X  X      |          |X  X      |          ||
|X  X      |          |X  X      |          ||
|X  X      |          |X  X      |          ||
|X  X      |          |X  X      |          ||
|X  X      |          |X  X      |          ||
|X  X      |          |0  X      |          ||
 1  2-3-4~1-2-3-4     1  2-3-4~1-2-3-4
```

Notice how the **~** symbol connects notes in measures *A* and B, and in measures *C* and D. The first note in measures *A* and *C* get just 1 count. The second note in measures *A* and *C* are blown, then held for 7 counts as it extends into its next measure.

A *B*
one [two three four ~ one two three four]
---Hold across the ~ for 7 counts---

C *D*
one [two three four ~ one two three four]
---Hold across the ~ for 7 counts---

This next example also illustrates the tied note from one measure to the next, but the tune is a bit more complex.

Baby Chant #5: Play straight through, A - D.

```
A          B         C          D
|X X X  |     X X|X X    X|X X X   ||
|X X X  |     X X|X X    X|X X X   ||
|X X X  |     X X|X X    X|X X X   ||
|X 0 X  |     X X|X X    X|X X X   ||
|X 0 X  |     X X|0 X    X|X X X   ||
|X 0 0  |     X X|0 0    X|0 X X   ||
 1 2 3-4~1-2  3 4 1 2-3  4 1 2 3-4
```

A *B*
one two [three four ~ one two] three four
[Hold across the ~ for 4 counts]

C *D*
one two three four ~ one two three four

These baby chants might seem rather abstract to you right now. But when you begin applying the duration values to more tunes, you will intuitively know how to apply the numbers as well as other symbols to each note.

-Chapter 5-

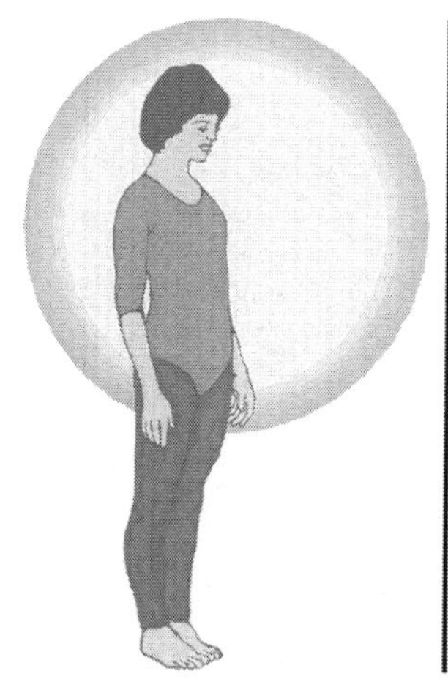

First Steps

Pentatonic Scale
Familiar Tunes
Easy Chants

Even if you've never had a music lesson, you probably have a pretty good idea of what they must be like. The devoted musician loves to practice scales and exercises. But not everyone is a devoted musician. That's why the tunes in this book are not scales and exercises. The tunes are standalone tunes, simple at the outset, but gradually becoming more challenging, (not difficult, but challenging), as you move through the material. Even the first "Lotus Chants" in this First-Steps section make good meditative tunes.

HALF BEATS: Also in this section we will further explore the duration symbol that assigns a half beat to a note. We will quickly see how this works with the familiar tune, Skip to My Lou.

-LOTUS CHANTS-

Lotus Chant #1: A - D, play through twice

```
A               B             C              D
|X  X  X  X  |X X   X   |X X   X    |X X    X  ||
|X  X  X  X  |X X   X   |X X   X    |X X    X  ||
|X  X  X  X  |X X   X   |X X   X    |X X    X  ||
|X  X  X  0  |X X   X   |X 0   X    |X X    X  ||
|X  X  0  0  |0 X   X   |X 0   0    |X X    X  ||
|X  0  0  0  |0 0   X   |X 0   0    |0 X    X  ||
 1  2  3  4   1 2  3-4   1 2  3-4    1 2   3-4
```

This chant is very easy to play. Just make *note* of the last note in measures B, C, and D. This third note is held for 2 counts.

Lotus Chant #2: A - D

```
 A            B           C            D
|X    X X  |X          |X    X X  |X          ||
|X    X X  |X          |X    X X  |X          ||
|X    X X  |X          |X    X X  |X          ||
|X    X X  |X          |0    X 0  |X          ||
|X    X 0  |X          |0    0 0  |X          ||
|X    0 0  |X          |0    0 0  |X          ||
 1-2  3 4   1-2-3-4     1-2  3 4   1-2-3-4
```

In measure *A* the first note is held through 2 counts (1-2). The second note is held for 1 count (3), as is the third note (4). In measure *B* the single note is blown once and held (continue blowing) through 4 counts (1-2-3-4). In measure *C* the first note is held for 2 counts (1-2) while the second and third note is each held for 1 count, (3) and (4). In measure *D* the note is blown once and is held through 4 counts (1-2-3-4).

Lotus Chant #3: A - D

```
 A          B          C         D
|X X    X |X X X   |X X X   |X 0 0   ||
|X 0    X |X X X   |X X X   |0 X X   ||
|X X    X |X X X   |X X X   |X 0 0   ||
|X 0    0 |X X X   |X 0 0   |0 0 0   ||
|X 0    0 |X X X   |0 0 0   |0 0 0   ||
|X 0    0 |0 X X   |0 0 0   |0 0 0   ||
 1 2-3  4  1 2 3-4  1 2 3-4  1 2 3-4
```

Measure *A* is just a tiny bit tricky. The first note is 1 count (1), but the second note is held through 2 counts (2-3) and the third note is 1 count (4). The rest of the tune is easy.

Lotus Chant #4: Tied Note in measure B into measure C. Play A - D.

```
A          B          C           D
|X    X   |X X        |          X|X X X      ||
|X    X   |X X        |          X|X X X      ||
|X    X   |X X        |          X|X X X      ||
|X    0   |X 0        |          X|X X X      ||
|X    0   |0 0        |          0|X X X      ||
|X    0   |0 0        |          0|0 X X      ||
 1-2 3-4 1 2-3-4~1-2-3 4 1 2 3-4
```

In this tune we hold notes from one measure to the next, so be alert for the ~ symbol. Think of that wonky little tilde symbol, ~, as being like a bridge into the next measure. When you see the symbol '~' at the end of a measure, you know that the note is to be held into the next measure.

It would be a good idea to take a breath at the beginning of measure B. That gives you enough air to hold that second note in measure B into measure C for the full 6 counts, and still have enough air to continue to the end.

Lotus Chant #5:

Play Order: [A]2x, B, C, [A]2x, C, D

```
A        B        C        D
|X X X X|X X X X|X 0 0 0|0 X X   ||
|X X X X|X X X X|0 X X X|X X X   ||
|X X X X|X X X X|X 0 0 0|0 X X   ||
|X X X X|X 0 0 0|0 0 0 0|0 0 X   ||
|X X X X|0 0 0 0|0 0 0 0|0 0 X   ||
|0 X X X|0 0 0 0|0 0 0 0|0 0 X   ||
 1 2 3 4 1 2 3 4 1 2 3 4 1 2 3-4
```

A straightforward way of writing the playing order where we *repeat some of the measures* would be to show a measure letter more than once. The playing order in this tune then would be — A, A, B, C, A, A, C, D

A simpler notation would be [A]2x, B, C, [A]2x, C, D, using 2x to mean a measure, or maybe a group of measures, to be played twice. This 2x repeat symbol will come in handy in more complex tunes, and we will use this simpler notation because it's more compact as well as clearer.

The playing order in this tune is simple. Play measure A twice, before moving on. Then play measure B once, then measure C once. Now you've played through the tune one time. Now we go back and again play measure A twice, then skip measure B and play C, and finally end with measure D and a nice long sustain on the last note to end the tune.

You can play this tune slow and meditatively, or you can play it fast like a dance. You are the creator!

NOTES THAT RECEIVE 1/2 COUNT

Lotus Chant #6: Play straight through.

```
 A           B              C
 |X X X X    |X X X X X     |X X X X    ||
 |X X X X    |X X X X X     |X X X X    ||
 |X X X X    |X X X X X     |X X X X    ||
 |X X X X    |X X X X X     |X X 0 X    ||
 |X X 0 X    |X X X 0 X     |X 0 0 X    ||
 |X 0 0 X    |0 X X 0 X     |0 0 0 X    ||
  1 2 & 3-4   1 & 2 & 3-4    1 & 2 3-4
```

Let's try one more lotus chant. This example will help us understand the **&** symbol. Remember, when a "**&**" follows a number, each of those two notes gets 1/2 count.

The tune on the next page is the American folk tune, "Skip to My Lou". If it's familiar to you, play through it without looking at the duration numbers below the notes. Once you are comfortable in playing the tune smoothly, play through it again several times, but look at the duration numbers as you play each note. You will immediately see that the duration numbers match the rhythm of the tune exactly. Matching the duration number to each note will show you what all those **&** symbols really mean.

Skip to My Lou: A - H

```
A                      B                 C
|X   X X X   X X|X   X X 0   |X   X X X   X X|
|X   X X X   X X|X   X X X   |X   X X X   X X|
|0   0 0 X   X X|0   0 0 0   |X   X X X   X X|
|0   0 0 X   X X|0   0 0 0   |0   0 0 X   X X|
|0   0 0 0   0 0|0   0 0 0   |0   0 0 0   0 0|
|0   0 0 0   0 0|0   0 0 0   |0   0 0 X   X X|
 1   2 & 3   4 & 1   2 & 3-4 1   2 & 3   4 &

D                E                   F
|X   X X X   |X   X X X   X X |X   X X 0   |
|X   X X 0   |X   X X X   X X |X   X X X   |
|X   X X X   |0   0 0 X   X X |0   0 0 0   |
|0   0 0 0   |0   0 0 X   X X |0   0 0 0   |
|0   0 0 0   |0   0 0 0   0 0 |0   0 0 0   |
|0   0 0 0   |0   0 0 0   0 0 |0   0 0 0   |
 1   2 & 3-4 1   2 & 3   4 &  1   2 & 3-4

G                H
|X   X X X   X |X     X    ||
|X   X 0 X   X |X     X    ||
|X   0 X 0   X |X     X    ||
|0   0 0 0   0 |X     X    ||
|0   0 0 0   0 |0     0    ||
|0   0 0 0   0 |0     0    ||
 1   2 & 3   4  1-2   3-4
```

Notice the '**&**' characters in this TAB. The '&' means the note gets 1/2 count, not 1 count. If an "&" symbol *follows* a duration number, it means *both* the numbered note and the note with the "&" symbol gets a half beat

```
Lotus Chant 7: A, B, C, B, D, B, [E]2x

A          B          C
|X X     X|X X X    |0      X X|
|0 X     X|X X X    |X      X X|
|X X     X|X X X    |0      X X|
|0 0     X|X 0 0    |0      0 X|
|0 0     X|0 0 0    |0      0 X|
|0 0     0|0 0 0    |0      0 0|
 1 2-3   4 1 2 3-4   1-2    3 4

D          E
|X     0 X|X X   X   X    ||
|0     X X|X X   X   X    ||
|X     0 X|X X   X   X    ||
|0     0 0|X X   X   X    ||
|0     0 0|0 X   X   X    ||
|0     0 0|0 0   X   X    ||
 1-2   3 4 1 &   2   3-4
```

When referring to the playing order, notice that measure B is used three different times in this tune. Do you see the "1 &" duration numbers at the beginning of measure E? Recall that this means both the '1' and the '&' get a half beat each. As you *silently* count the rhythm, say "one and".

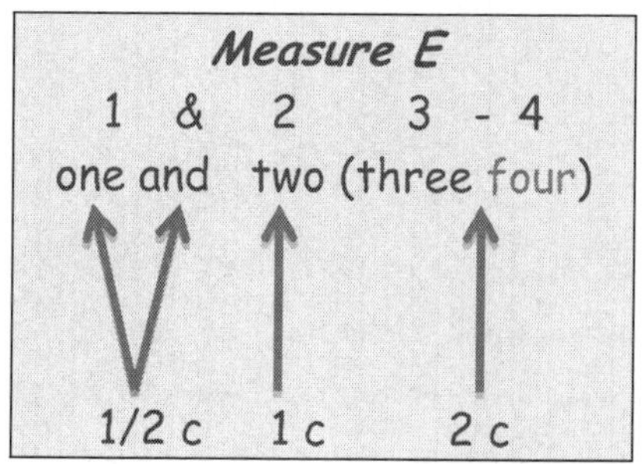

- PICKUP Notes-

The PICKUP note shows up in many tunes. Simply put, the pickup note, or sometimes notes, introduces the first *main* melody note.

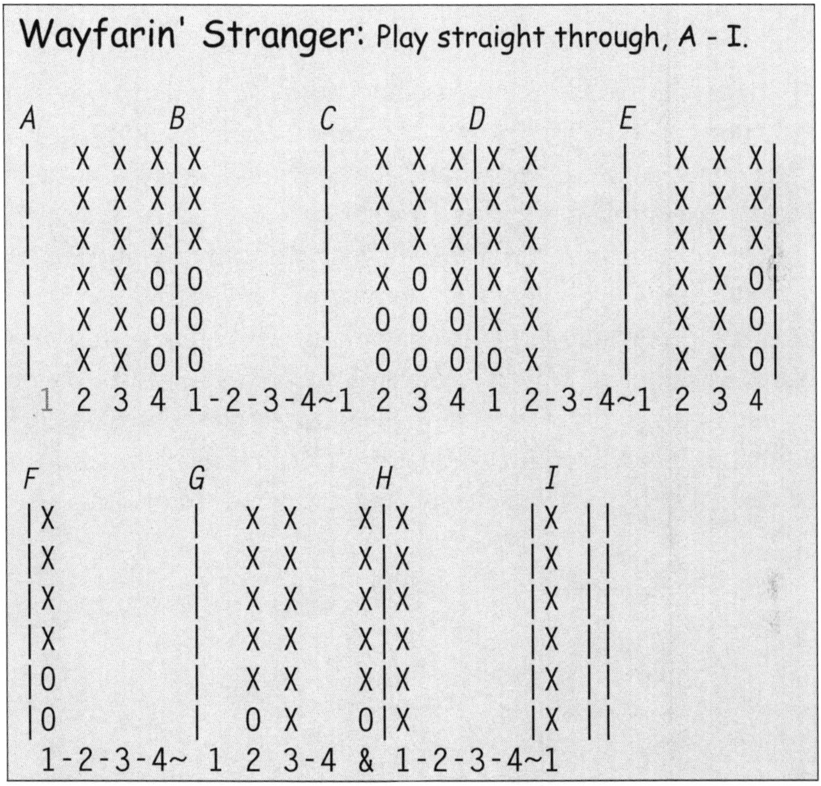

Wayfarin' Stranger: Play straight through, A - I.

```
A        B                C         D                E
|  X X X|X                |  X X X|X X               |  X X X|
|  X X X|X                |  X X X|X X               |  X X X|
|  X X X|X                |  X X X|X X               |  X X X|
|  X X 0|0                |  X 0 X|X X               |  X X 0|
|  X X 0|0                |  0 0 0|X X               |  X X 0|
|  X X 0|0                |  0 0 0|0 X               |  X X 0|
 1 2 3 4 1-2-3-4~1 2 3 4 1 2-3-4~1 2 3 4

F        G            H          I
|X       |  X X    X|X        |X ||
|X       |  X X    X|X        |X ||
|X       |  X X    X|X        |X ||
|X       |  X X    X|X        |X ||
|0       |  X X    X|X        |X ||
|0       |  0 X    0|X        |X ||
 1-2-3-4~ 1 2 3-4 & 1-2-3-4~1
```

A perfect example of a tune that uses pickup notes is "Wayfarin' Stranger". This tune has four beats to each measure. Notice the one grayed out duration number, '1', in the first measure, measure A. The gray number means there is an *invisible* note that gets one beat, but the beat is heard in our mind, not played on the flute. The three pickup notes are played on '2', '3', and '4'. If we would sing along, these three pickup notes would be on the word's, "I'm just a", the first three words in the lyrics.

```
  I'm just a  poooooor   way fa-rin' stran-ger......      travel-in'
1  2    3  4 1-2-3-4~1   2   3   4      1     2-3-4~1-2  3    4

Through    this world of woe...........
 1-2-3-4~1  2    3     4  1-2-3-4~1
```

This TAB is for just the last section of this great tune. **The tune in its entirety** is at the end of the book, page 142, in the bonus tune section where you will find the more difficult pieces. Nevertheless, this short section is a wonderful meditative tune that's well within your skill range right now.

Folk tunes are great fun to play on the Native American flute. It's especially fun to play those folk tunes that have haunting melodies. If you would like to turn your flute playing to folk tunes, both American as well as world folk tunes, you might be interested in my Native American flute tutorial package, "Earth Flute". You can find out more about it at—

FluteFlights.com

-First and Second Endings-

Lotus Chant 8: A - E, B - D, F.

```
A       B       C       D
|      X|X   X X|X     X|X   X X|
|      X|X   X X|X     X|X   X X|
|      X|X   X X|X     X|X   X X|
|      X|X   X X|X     X|X   0 X|
|      X|0   X 0|X     X|0   0 X|
|      X|0   0 0|X     X|0   0 0|
 1 2 3 4 1-2 3 4 1-2-3 4 1-2 3 4

E       F
|X     X|X    ||
|X     X|X    ||
|X     X|X    ||
|X     X|X    ||
|0     X|0    ||
|0     X|0    ||
 1-2-3 4 1-2-3
```

Playing Order: Play measure A *through* measure E. **Measure E is the first ending.** Next, go back and play measures B through D. (Notice we skip measure A the second time through.) Finally, play measure F to end the tune. **Measure F is the second ending.**

In measure A we see the three grayed out duration numbers, 1, 2, and 3. No notes are played with these numbers, but we count them silently to ourselves. The fourth duration number is a played note, and this is the pickup note. A pickup note, (or sometimes note*s*), serves to start off a tune, but it doesn't appear as the first note of the first measure like one would expect. It always falls somewhere *after* the first note in the first measure, the pickup measure, and then the main part of the melody proceeds in earnest at the beginning of the second measure. You've heard pickup notes many times in all kinds of music, but you probably didn't know they were there. Nevertheless, the pickup note is an important concept, and we will be using pickup notes throughout the rest of this book.

Watch that 2nd ending at measure F. Measure E is the 1st ending and we skip this ending the second time through to finish with measure F, the 2nd ending. Many songs use 1st and 2nd endings.

Lotus Chant #9: A - C, B, D

```
A         B               C
|        X|X  X X  X  X X|X  X X  X    X|
|        X|X  X X  X  X X|X  X X  X    X|
|        X|X  X X  X  X X|X  X X  X    X|
|        X|X  0 X  X  X X|X  X X  X    X|
|        X|0  0 0  X  X X|0  0 X  0    X|
|        X|0  0 0  0  X 0|0  0 0  0    X|
 1 2 3 4 & 1  2 &  3  4 & 1  2 &  3-4  &

D
|X  X X  X   ||
|X  X X  X   ||
|X  X X  X   ||
|X  X X  X   ||
|0  0 X  0   ||
|0  0 0  0   ||
 1  2 &  3-4
```

Notice that the pickup note in measure A is just a half beat. The note is played on the '&', not on the '4'.

In this tune the first ending is measure C, which we play from A to C. The second time through we start at measure B, skip C, and jump to D. Measure D is the second ending. As you work your way through these tunes, you will come to see why a second ending is sometimes necessary.

-Chapter 6-

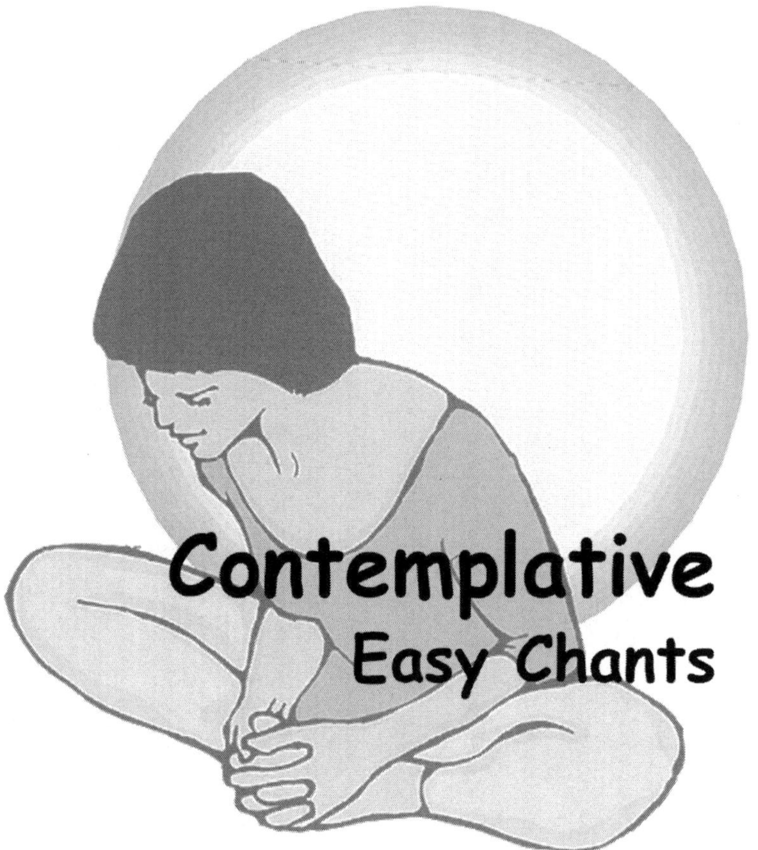

Contemplative Easy Chants

The following set of chants are named, or at least inspired, by actual yoga pose names. The first chant is titled "Downward Dog". Even beginner yoga students are familiar with this pose. The pose is easy and so is the chant.

Another chant titled "Little Thunderbolt" is an advanced backbend pose that's not for the faint of heart! But unlike the pose, the chant is easy.

Downward Dog: [A - D]3x

```
A          B          C         D
|X X X    |X X X X|X    X X|X        ||
|X X X    |0 X X X|X    X X|X        ||
|X X X    |X X X X|X    X X|X        ||
|X 0 0    |0 0 X X|X    X X|X        ||
|X 0 0    |0 0 0 X|X    X X|X        ||
|X 0 0    |0 0 0 0|X    0 X|X        ||
 1 2 3-4 1 2 3 4 1-2 3 4 1-2-3-4
```

The *Downward-Facing Dog* pose is probably the most recognized of all the yoga poses. If you practice yoga, you have done this pose many times, and you know what an invigorating stretch this pose can be. The tune above can give you that same easy stretch. In measure A we start at the lowest note, then *stretch* musically upward through the first note in measure B. Then we slowly come back down the scale, finally ending on the lowest note in measure D, the last measure. Nice stretch!

Play measures A through D and repeat the tune three times, (or more!). Sometimes the most basic poses and basic tunes can be the most beneficial. Just ease through the tune, much as you would ease through the pose.

Little Thunderbolt: [A]3x, B, [C]2x, A, D

```
 A         B         C         D
|X X X X X|X X X X X|X X X X X|X X X X   ||
|X X X X X|X X X X X|0 X X X X|X X X X   ||
|X X X X X|X X X X X|X X X X X|X X X X   ||
|X X X X X|X 0 0 0 0|0 0 0 0 0|X X X X   ||
|X X X X X|0 0 0 0 0|0 0 0 0 0|0 X X X   ||
|0 X X X X|0 0 0 0 0|0 0 0 0 0|0 0 X X   ||
 1 & 2 3 4 1 & 2 3 4 1 & 2 3 4 1 & 2 3-4
```

This is a repetitive tune, which makes it fun to play. Notice how measure A is repeated three times. Measure B is played only once, measure C is played twice, then back to measure A once and measure D once to end. Notice the "1 &" duration numbers at the beginning of each measure. The cadence is like you might hear on a tom-tom. Repeat as often as you like. If you want to use this particular tune to meditate to, play it slowly and with feeling. Visualize a little thunderbolt slowly crackling above you in a summer rain. If you want to make it sound like a dance, play it faster, as if thunderbolts are crashing to the ground at your very feet! You are the artist. You are the interpreter of your own heart, and the tunes you play will reflect that part of you.

Bird of Paradise: [A, B, C, B]2x

```
A        B                    C
|X X X   |X X X X X X X|0 X X   ||
|X 0 X   |X 0 X X X X X|X X X   ||
|X X X   |X X X X X X X|0 X X   ||
|X 0 0   |X 0 0 X X 0 0|0 0 0   ||
|X 0 0   |X 0 0 X 0 0 0|0 0 0   ||
|X 0 0   |X 0 0 0 0 0 0|0 0 0   ||
 1 2 3-4  1 & 2 & 3 & 4 1 2 3-4
```

This easy chant sounds like a singing bird. In the playing order, I suggest you play the chant two times, but you can play it as many times as you want. Sometimes we get the most benefit if we repeat the tune many times, like a mantra. Notice that by playing measure B last, the tune ends like a question. This adds mystery and depth to the chant. It's almost as if the bird is twittering, "Hey, I'm here. What are you gonna do about it?"

Be especially aware of the half beat notes in measure B. Also notice that the last note with duration number "4", is not followed by an & symbol, like the other beat numbers are. So that last note, (4), in measure B, is one whole beat. All the other notes in measure B are 1/2 beat.

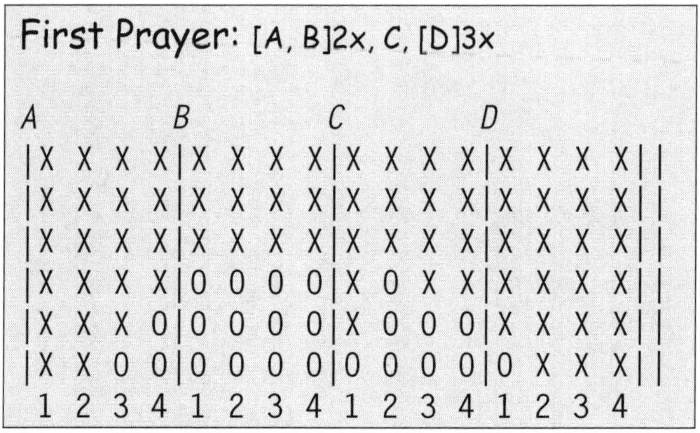

First Prayer: [A, B]2x, C, [D]3x

```
A         B         C         D
|X X X X|X X X X|X X X X|X X X X||
|X X X X|X X X X|X X X X|X X X X||
|X X X X|X X X X|X X X X|X X X X||
|X X X X|0 0 0 0|X 0 X X|X X X X||
|X X X 0|0 0 0 0|X 0 0 0|X X X X||
|X X 0 0|0 0 0 0|0 0 0 0|0 X X X||
 1 2 3 4 1 2 3 4 1 2 3 4 1 2 3 4
```

I seldom repeat tunes from one book to another in my flute series of books, but I very occasionally make an exception if the tune is universal in reaching across all my books. This tune, "First Prayer", is one such tune. You'll notice that the melody is straightforward, with each note having the same duration of one count. There are no tied notes, no pickup notes, and no '&' notes that receive a half a beat. But it demonstrates the beauty of a simple tune, and that's why I include the tune in this book.

Do not play this tune from measure A to measure D. Notice the path after the title. Play measures A through B twice. Play measure C just once, and play measure D three times. Of course, you can repeat the whole tune as many times as you wish. Tongue each note and play it at a slow to moderate tempo (speed).

```
Happy Baby: [A - D]2x, A, B.

A       B                   C
|X X X  |X X X X X X X|X 0 X   |
|X 0 X  |X X X X X X X|0 X X   |
|X X X  |X X X X X X X|X 0 X   |
|X 0 0  |X X 0 X X X X|0 0 0   |
|X 0 0  |X 0 0 0 X X X|0 0 0   |
|X 0 0  |0 0 0 0 0 X X|0 0 0   |
 1 2 3-4 1 & 2 & 3 & 4 1 2 3-4

D
|X X X X X 0 0|
|X X X X 0 X X|
|X X X X X 0 0|
|X X X 0 0 0 0|
|0 X 0 0 0 0 0|
|0 0 0 0 0 0 0|
 1 & 2 & 3 & 4
```

Repeat A through D two times, then A, then B, the ending measure in this chant. A nice way to play this tune is to gradually slow down to end, as if you are gradually applying the brakes when you drive up to a Stop sign, finally trilling the bottom note hole, (rapidly opening and closing the bottom note hole), on the very last note in measure B, which is the last measure to be played in the tune.

This is a happy tune that should be played joyfully! Imagine yourself talking to a little baby with your flute. Let the baby gurgle happily through your flute, and let the baby fall asleep by slowing down at the ending.

Melting Heart: [A - D]2x, [E - H]2x

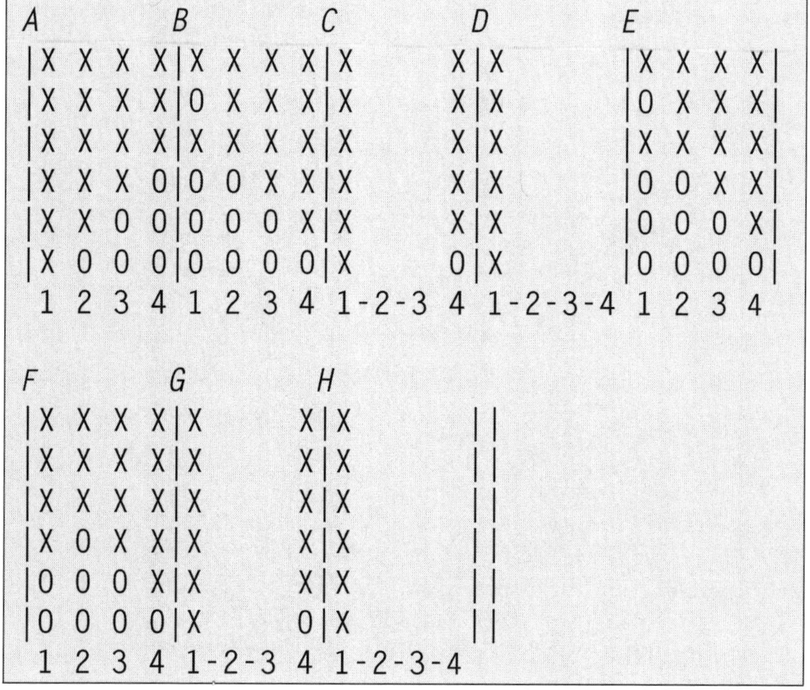

```
 A        B        C         D         E
|X X X X|X X X X|X       X|X       |X X X X|
|X X X X|0 X X X|X       X|X       |0 X X X|
|X X X X|X X X X|X       X|X       |X X X X|
|X X X 0|0 0 X X|X       X|X       |0 0 X X|
|X X 0 0|0 0 0 X|X       X|X       |0 0 0 X|
|X 0 0 0|0 0 0 0|X       0|X       |0 0 0 0|
 1 2 3 4 1 2 3 4 1-2-3 4 1-2-3-4 1 2 3 4

 F        G         H
|X X X X|X       X|X       ||
|X X X X|X       X|X       ||
|X X X X|X       X|X       ||
|X 0 X X|X       X|X       ||
|0 0 0 X|X       X|X       ||
|0 0 0 0|X       0|X       ||
 1 2 3 4 1-2-3 4 1-2-3-4
```

Since the purpose of the yoga pose, "Melting Heart", is to open the heart in a relaxed way, we can convey that concept and feeling in the way we play this tune. Simply blow as long a breath as you can, but finger each note as this continuous stream of air powers your flute. Do not try to alter the notes with tonguing or the tremolo. Simply let each note smoothly slip from the flute as you blow a long, steady breath. Of course, you will have to take a breath now and again. But you can do this smoothly with a bit of practice. Two good places to take a breath are at the last note in measure C and the last note in measure G. Although simple to play, this is a beautiful, smooth sounding tune to begin your meditation sessions with.

Half Moon: A - **I**, B - H, **J**

```
A       B       C       D       E
|      X|X   X  |      X|X X X X|X     X|
|      X|0   X  |      X|X X X X|X     X|
|      X|X   X  |      X|X X X X|X     X|
|      X|0   0  |      X|X 0 0 X|0     X|
|      X|0   0  |      X|0 0 0 0|0     X|
|      X|0   0  |      0|0 0 0 0|0     X|
 1 2 3 4 1-2 3-4~1-2-3 4 1 2 3 4 1-2-3 4

F       G       H       I       J
|0   X  |      X|X X X X|X     X|X    ||
|X   X  |      X|X X X X|X     X|X    ||
|0   X  |      X|X X X X|X     X|X    ||
|0   0  |      X|X X X X|X     X|X    ||
|0   0  |      0|X X X X|X     X|X    ||
|0   0  |      0|0 X X 0|X     X|X    ||
 1-2 3-4~1-2-3 4 1 2 3 4 1-2-3 4 1-2-3
```

Play A through I. **I** is the first ending. Play B through H, but skip I, the 1st ending, and instead play **J**, the 2nd ending.

Notice the three gray notes in measure A. These notes help you silently count off the first three beats in measure A, coming in on the first blown note, the pickup note, at the 4 count. Also notice the ~ symbol at the end of measures B and F. The ~ indicates the note is blown in these measures and then held into the next measure.

-Chapter 7-

7 Daily Rhythmic Chants

Following are seven chants, Monday through Sunday. None of the chants are difficult, but pay attention to the duration numbers below each note. There is much variety in these seven chants, and we want to play them correctly.

Mountain (Monday): [A - D]2x

```
A          B          C          D
|X X    X|X X X  |X X X  |X X X    ||
|X X    X|X X X  |X X X  |X X X    ||
|X X    X|X X X  |X X X  |X X X    ||
|X X    X|X X X  |X X X  |X X X    ||
|X X    X|X 0 X  |X X X  |0 X X    ||
|X X    X|0 0 X  |0 X X  |0 X X    ||
 1 2-3 4 1 2 3-4 1 2 3-4 1 2 3-4
```

Play this tune slowly and ponderously, like a mountain, like the yoga pose.

Garland (Tuesday) - [A -B] 2x

```
A                 B
|X X  X X  X  X|X X  X  X X  X||
|X X  X X  X  X|X X  X  X X  X||
|X 0  X X  X  X|0 X  X  X X  X||
|X X  0 X  X  X|X X  X  X X  X||
|0 0  0 0  X  X|0 0  0  X 0  0||
|0 0  0 0  X  X|0 0  0  0 0  0||
 1 &  2 &  3  4 1 &  2  3 &  4
```

Pay special attention to the "new" note. It occurs as the second note in measure A, as well as the first note in measure B. Since the note exists in the complete **chromatic scale,** (page 36, note #8), the note isn't new, even though we haven't used this note in a tune before.

```
Heron (Wednesday): [A - D] 2x

A       B                    C        D
|X X   X|X X X X   X   |X 0   X|X 0 0   0   ||
|X X   X|X X X X   X   |0 X   X|0 X X   X   ||
|X X   X|X X X X   X   |X 0   X|X 0 0   0   ||
|X 0   X|X 0 X X   X   |0 0   0|0 0 0   0   ||
|X 0   X|0 0 0 X   X   |0 0   0|0 0 0   0   ||
|X 0   0|0 0 0 0   X   |0 0   0|0 0 0   0   ||
 1 2-3 4 1 & 2 &  3-4 1 2-3 4 1 & 2  3-4
```

Just as the Heron pose has two distinct stages of execution, the Heron chant has two stages with measures A, B stage one and measures C, D stage two.

```
Handstand Chant (Thursday) - [A, B] 2x

A       B
|0 X   X|0 X X X   X   ||
|X X   X|X X X X   X   ||
|0 X   X|0 X X X   X   ||
|0 X   0|0 0 X 0   X   ||
|0 X   0|0 0 0 0   X   ||
|0 X   0|0 0 0 0   X   ||
 1 2-3 4 1 & 2 &  3-4
```

At first it might be difficult to close all holes as we move from note 1 to note 2-3 in measure A. But with a bit of practice this will nicely fall into place. Take this tune very, very slowly until closing all those notes from a previous note becomes second nature. Notice how this chant sounds like it's going upside down, just as if you were performing a hand stand.

Crescent Moon (Friday): [A - D] 2x

```
A           B             C             D
|X X    X|X X X        |0 X X X   |X X       ||
|X 0    X|X X X        |X X X X   |X X       ||
|X X    X|X X X        |0 X X X   |X X       ||
|0 0    0|X X X        |0 0 X X   |X X       ||
|0 0    0|0 X X        |0 0 X X   |X X       ||
|0 0    0|0 0 X        |0 0 0 X   |0 X       ||
 1 2-3 4 1 & 2-3-4 1 & 2 3-4 1 2-3-4
```

Tree Chant (Saturday): [A - B] 2x

```
A                       B
|X X X X X X X X|X X X X X   ||
|X X 0 X X X X X|X X X X X   ||
|X 0 X 0 X X X X|X X X X X   ||
|X X 0 X X X X X|X 0 X X X   ||
|0 0 0 0 0 X X X|0 0 0 X 0   ||
|0 0 0 0 0 0 X 0|0 0 0 0 0   ||
 1 & 2 & 3 & 4 & 1 & 2 & 3-4
```

Compass (Sunday): [A - D] 2x

```
A         B          C             D
|0    X  |X    X   |X X X X   X|X 0      ||
|X    X  |X    X   |X X X X   X|0 X      ||
|0    X  |X    X   |X X X X   X|X 0      ||
|0    0  |X    X   |X X X X   X|0 0      ||
|0    0  |0    X   |0 0 X X   X|0 0      ||
|0    0  |0    X   |0 0 0 X   X|0 0      ||
 1-2 3-4 1-2 3-4 1 2 3 &   4 1 2-3-4
```

-Chapter 8-

There are 12 poses to the whole Sun Salutation (Surya Namaskar) routine. I have written a short chant for each pose. You can repeat each chant as often as you like. All the chants are musically related in one big 12-part flute salutation. So once you can comfortably play all the chants, you can play each chant from Chant #1 through Chant #12, one after the other, to make one long chant. You can also play the chants in various orders and combinations to compose your own long chants.

Repeat each chant as many times as you like.

STEP 1: Mountain Pose. Bring palms together in prayer position. Exhale.

Sun Salutation #1: [A - B]

```
A        B
|X X    X|X X   X   X    ||
|X X    X|X X   X   X    ||
|X X    X|X X   X   X    ||
|X X    X|X X   X   X    ||
|X X    X|X 0   X   X    ||
|X X    X|0 0   X   X    ||
 1 2-3  4 1 &   2   3-4
```

STEP 2: Inhale, raise arms overhead, palms together.

Sun Salutation #2: [A - B]

```
A        B
|X X    X|X X   X   X    ||
|X X    X|X X   X   X    ||
|X X    X|X X   X   X    ||
|X 0    X|X 0   0   0    ||
|0 0    X|0 0   0   0    ||
|0 0    0|0 0   0   0    ||
 1 2-3  4 1 &   2   3-4
```

STEP 3: Exhale and bend forward until hands touch feet.

Sun Salutation #3: [A - B]

```
A                  B
|0 X  X X  X X  X X|X X X X   ||
|X 0  X X  X X  X X|X X X X   ||
|0 X  X X  X X  X X|X X X X   ||
|0 0  0 X  X 0  X X|X X X X   ||
|0 0  0 X  0 0  0 X|X X X X   ||
|0 0  0 0  0 0  0 0|X 0 X X   ||
 1 &  2 &  3 &  4 & 1 2 & 3-4
```

STEP 4: Inhale, step right leg back, arch back and lift chin.

Sun Salutation #4: [A - B]

```
A              B
|X X  X  X X  X|X X  X  X   ||
|X X  X  X X  X|X X  X  X   ||
|X X  X  X X  X|X X  X  X   ||
|X X  X  X X  X|X 0  X  X   ||
|X X  X  0 X  X|0 0  X  X   ||
|0 X  X  0 X  X|0 0  0  X   ||
 1 &  2  3 &  4 1 &  2  3-4
```

STEP 5: Exhaling, step left leg back into plank position. Keep spine and legs in a straight line and support your weight on hands and feet.

```
Sun Salutation #5: [A - B]

A         B
|X X    X|X X   X   X   |
|0 X    X|X X   X   X   |
|X X    X|X X   X   X   |
|0 0    0|X X   X   X   |
|0 0    0|0 X   X   X   |
|0 0    0|0 0   X   X   |
 1 2-3  4 1 &   2   3-4
```

STEP 6: Retaining the breath, lower knees, chest and then forehead; keep hips up and toes curled under.

```
Sun Salutation #6: [A - B]

A                 B
|X X   X   X   |X X   X   X   ||
|X X   X   X   |X X   X   X   ||
|X X   X   X   |X X   X   X   ||
|X 0   X   X   |X X   X   X   ||
|0 0   X   X   |0 X   X   X   ||
|0 0   0   X   |0 0   X   X   ||
 1 &   2   3-4  1 &   2   3-4
```

STEP 7: Inhaling, stretch forward and bend back. Keep arms straight.

```
Sun Salutation #7: [A - B]

A                B
|X X  X  X X  X|X X  X X  0   ||
|0 X  X  X X  X|0 X  X 0  X   ||
|X X  X  X X  X|X X  X X  0   ||
|0 0  0  X X  X|0 0  0 0  0   ||
|0 0  0  X X  X|0 0  0 0  0   ||
|0 0  0  0 X  X|0 0  0 0  0   ||
 1 &  2  3 &  4 1 &  2 &  3-4
```

STEP 8: Exhaling, curl your toes under, press down into your heels, and lift your hips.

```
Sun Salutation #8: [A - B]

A        B
|X X X X|X 0  0 X  0   ||
|X X X X|0 X  X X  X   ||
|X X X X|X 0  0 X  0   ||
|X X X X|0 0  0 0  0   ||
|X X 0 X|0 0  0 0  0   ||
|0 X 0 X|0 0  0 0  0   ||
 1 2 3 4 1 &  2 &  3-4
```

STEP 9: As you inhale, bring right leg forward, with top of foot stretched out flat on floor; lift your chin.

Sun Salutation #9: [A - B]

```
A                   B
|X X  X  X X  X|0 X  X X  X   ||
|X X  X  X X  X|X X  X 0  X   ||
|X X  X  X X  X|0 X  X X  X   ||
|0 X  X  X X  X|0 0  0 0  X   ||
|0 X  0  0 X  X|0 0  0 0  X   ||
|0 0  0  0 X  X|0 0  0 0  X   ||
 1 &  2  3 &  4 1 &  2 &  3-4
```

STEP 10: Exhale and then bend forward until hands touch feet.

Sun Salutation #10: [A - B]

```
A                   B
|X X  X  X X  X|X 0  0  X 0  0||
|X X  X  X X  X|0 X  X  0 X  X||
|X X  X  X X  X|X 0  0  X 0  0||
|X X  X  X X  X|0 0  0  0 0  0||
|X X  X  X X  X|0 0  0  0 0  0||
|0 X  X  0 X  X|0 0  0  0 0  0||
 1 &  2  3 &  4 1 &  2  3 &  4
```

STEP 11: Inhaling, stretch arms forward and overhead. Slowly bend backward from waist.

```
Sun Salutation #11: [A -
B]

A           B
|X X    X|X X   X   X    ||
|0 X    X|X X   X   X    ||
|X X    X|X X   X   X    ||
|0 0    X|X X   X   X    ||
|0 0    X|0 X   X   X    ||
|0 0    0|0 X   X   X    ||
 1 2-3 4 1 &    2   3-4
```

STEP 12: Exhaling, gently come back to Mountain pose.

```
Sun Salutation #12: [A - B]

A           B
|X X    X|X X   X   X    ||
|X X    X|X X   X   X    ||
|X X    X|X X   X   X    ||
|X X    X|X 0   X   X    ||
|X X    X|0 0   X   X    ||
|X X    X|0 0   X   X    ||
 1 2-3 4 1 &    2   3-4
```

-Chapter 9-

Color Notes

Special notes that further expand the musical spectrum

Up to this point we have been using notes mostly from the extended Pentatonic scale. Since this book is about meditative chants on your flute, we will stay mainly within that extended Pentatonic range of notes. But if you have read through the reference material and studied the Chromatic Scale, (page 36), you already know there are even more useful notes on your Native American flute. I call the special three notes we will use in this section "color" notes. These three notes will add complexity and deeper dimension to your playing.

Adding these three notes to the eight notes of the extended Pentatonic scale gives us eleven notes to work with. There are four more notes in addition to the eleven, but those remaining four notes aren't necessary to keep us within the mystical feel of the chant. However, if you are interested in playing tunes that demand the whole 15 note scale, you can find them in any of my other Native American flute method ebook packages at FluteFlights.com.

We have been using the extended Pentatonic scale. That's this scale—

EXTENDED PENTATONIC SCALE:

```
X X X X X 0 0 0  |  0 0 0 X X X X X
X X X X 0 X 0 0  |  0 0 X 0 X X X X
X X X X X 0 0 0  |  0 0 0 X X X X X
X X X 0 0 0 0 0  |  0 0 0 0 0 X X X
X X 0 0 0 0 X X  |  X X 0 0 0 0 X X
X 0 0 0 0 0 X 0  |  0 X 0 0 0 0 0 X
Up the scale        Down the scale
```

We can add 3 useful notes to this scale, notes that will add interest and color.

ADDED *COLOR* NOTES:

```
      C     C   C
X X X X X X X 0 0 0 0
X X X X X 0 0 X 0 0 0
X X X X 0 X 0 0 0 0 0
X X X 0 X 0 0 0 0 0 0
X X 0 0 0 0 0 0 0 X X
X 0 0 0 0 0 0 0 0 X 0
```

The Cs in the top row show which notes are the new color notes. Notice the third *color note* (note #9) where no note holes are covered. Be careful not to blow this note too hard. This note is just one half step in pitch above the previous note, the octave note. If you blow this note too hard, it will sound "sharp", (sound higher than it should be).

Esteemed Guru: [A - B]2x, C

```
A                        B                     C
|X 0  0  0 0  0|0 X  X X  X   |X X  X  X ||
|0 X  X  0 X  X|X 0  0 X  X   |X X  X  X ||
|0 0  0  0 0  0|0 0  X X  X   |X X  X  X ||
|0 0  0  0 0  0|0 0  0 0  X   |X X  X  X ||
|0 0  0  0 0  0|0 0  0 0  0   |X 0  0  0 ||
|0 0  0  0 0  0|0 0  0 0  0   |0 0  0  0 ||
 1 &  2  3 &  4 1 &  2 &  3-4 1 &  2  3-4
```

Notice that the 4th note in measure A is all holes open. Be sure to blow this note gently. If you blow too hard, the note will sound too high, (sharp).

This is a strange sounding chant, but it will strengthen your repertoire of tunes. Once you play it a few times, it will sound more interesting than strange.

Crossbow: [A - B]2x, [C - D]2x, A, B

```
A          B                C
|X X X    |X X   X X   X   |X X   X      |
|X 0 0    |X 0   0 X   0   |X X   X      |
|X 0 X    |X 0   X X   X   |X 0   X      |
|X 0 0    |X 0   0 0   0   |X X   0      |
|X 0 0    |X 0   0 0   0   |0 0   0      |
|X 0 0    |X 0   0 0   0   |0 0   0      |
 1 2 3-4   1 &   2 &   3-4  1 &   2-3-4

D
|X X   X X   X   ||
|X X   X X   X   ||
|X 0   X X   X   ||
|X X   0 X   X   ||
|0 0   0 X   X   ||
|0 0   0 0   X   ||
 1 &   2 &   3-4
```

Named after the "bow pose", this is a strange piece I enjoyed composing. The first section, measures A and B, sounds quite different from the second section, measures C and D. Like the tension in a cross bow, there is musical tension in the last measure you play in this piece, measure B.

King Pidgeon: [A]3x, B, C

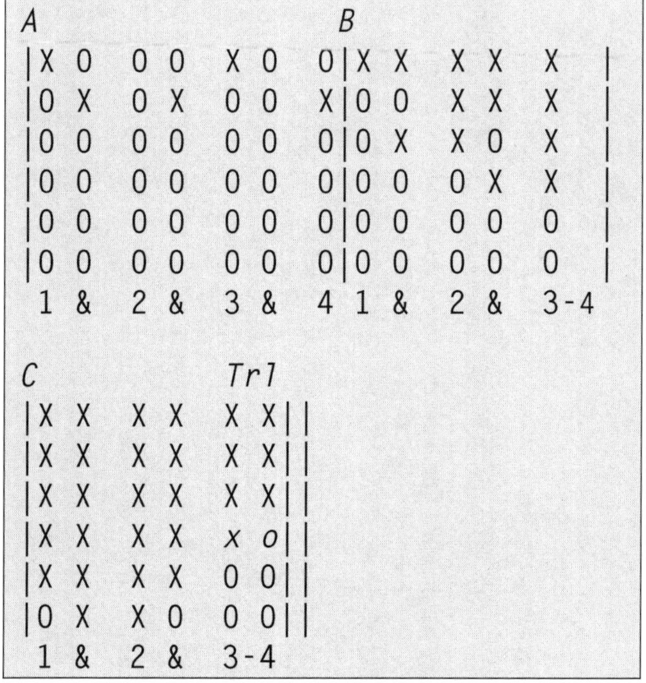

```
A                       B
|X 0  0 0  X 0  0|X X  X X  X   |
|0 X  0 X  0 0  X|0 0  X X  X   |
|0 0  0 0  0 0  0|0 X  X 0  X   |
|0 0  0 0  0 0  0|0 0  0 X  X   |
|0 0  0 0  0 0  0|0 0  0 0  0   |
|0 0  0 0  0 0  0|0 0  0 0  0   |
 1 &  2 &  3 &  4 1 &  2 &  3-4

C               Tr1
|X X  X X  X X||
|X X  X X  X X||
|X X  X X  X X||
|X X  X X  x o||
|X X  X X  0 0||
|0 X  X 0  0 0||
 1 &  2 &  3-4
```

The King Pidgeon yoga pose is a real back bender, requiring some care to get it right, much like the tune above. But like the pose, the more you play the tune, the easier it will become. Eventually the tune will make sense and it will be easy to play from memory. Just be very careful not to blow those color notes too hard. If you do, the pitch will go sharp, and then the melody will make little if any sense. Just take your time with it, practicing it very slowly at first and then gradually increasing the speed until it feels right. **Repeat the tune as many times as you like, but when playing it the last time, try trilling the last note in measure C to end.**

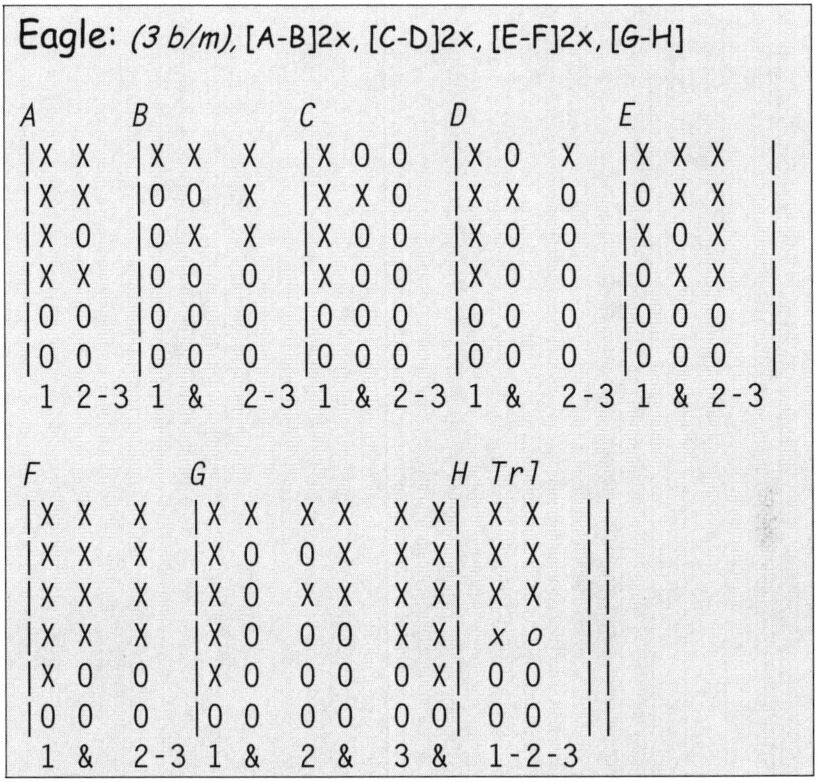

Eagle: *(3 b/m),* [A-B]2x, [C-D]2x, [E-F]2x, [G-H]

```
A       B           C          D           E
|X X    |X X   X    |X 0 0     |X 0   X    |X X X    |
|X X    |0 0   X    |X X 0     |X X   0    |0 X X    |
|X 0    |0 X   X    |X 0 0     |X 0   0    |X 0 X    |
|X X    |0 0   0    |X 0 0     |X 0   0    |0 X X    |
|0 0    |0 0   0    |0 0 0     |0 0   0    |0 0 0    |
|0 0    |0 0   0    |0 0 0     |0 0   0    |0 0 0    |
 1 2-3   1 &   2-3   1 & 2-3    1 &   2-3   1 & 2-3

F           G                  H Tr1
|X X   X    |X X   X X   X X|  X X    ||
|X X   X    |X 0   0 X   X X|  X X    ||
|X X   X    |X 0   X X   X X|  X X    ||
|X X   X    |X 0   0 0   X X|  x o    ||
|X 0   0    |X 0   0 0   0 X|  0 0    ||
|0 0   0    |0 0   0 0   0 0|  0 0    ||
 1 &   2-3   1 &   2 &   3 &   1-2-3
```

Even though I can't physically do the Eagle Pose, I think it's one of the more beautiful yoga poses, As the forearms intertwine, you can imagine the shape of an eagle's neck, head and beak in the pose.

Notice this tune is three beats to the measure. It's like a waltz. Play this majestic tune as you picture two people flying across the dance floor in a smooth waltz, or maybe two eagles with locked talons in a courtship dive. When you play measure H, you can warble off, (trill), the 3rd note from the bottom, to end. Rapidly open and close this hole, finally ending with the hole closed, just as you began.

(Notice the trill on the last note pair in measure H, the last measure.)

Peace Offering: [A-H]2x, I, J

```
A        B        C             D
|X    X X|0   X  |X 0 0 X  0  X|X X X X 0|
|X    X 0|X   X  |0 0 X 0  X  X|X X X 0 X|
|X    X X|0   X  |X 0 0 X  0  X|X X 0 0 0|
|X    0 0|0   0  |0 0 0 0  0  0|X 0 X 0 0|
|X    0 0|0   0  |0 0 0 0  0  0|0 0 0 0 0|
|X    0 0|0   0  |0 0 0 0  0  0|0 0 0 0 0|
 1-2  3 4 1-2 3-4 1 & 2 &  3  4 1 2 3 & 4

E             F              G
|X 0  X X  X  |X X  X  X  X X|X X  X X  |
|0 X  0 0  X  |X X  X  X  X X|X X  X X  |
|0 0  0 X  X  |0 X  X  X  X X|X X  X X  |
|0 0  0 0  0  |X 0  0  0  X 0|X X  X X  |
|0 0  0 0  0  |0 0  0  0  0 0|0 X  X X  |
|0 0  0 0  0  |0 0  0  0  0 0|0 0  X X  |
 1 &  2 &  3-4 1 &  2  3  4 & 1 &  2 3-4

H           I                 J  Tr1
|X X  X  X  |0 0  X X  X X  X X|  X X  ||
|X X  X  X  |0 X  0 0  X X  X X|  X X  ||
|X X  X  X  |0 0  0 X  0 0  X X|  X X  ||
|X X  X  X  |0 0  0 0  0 X  0 X|  X X  ||
|X X  X  X  |0 0  0 0  0 0  0 X|  X X  ||
|0 X  X  X  |0 0  0 0  0 0  0 0|  x o  ||
 1 &  2  3-4 1 &  2 &  3 &  4 &   1-2-3
```

Play this at a slow to medium speed. It's fun to play and there's a beautiful walk-down to end in measures I to J.

(Notice the trill in measure J.)

Prayer Wheels: [A-B]2x, [C-D]2x, E

```
A                      B
|  X   X X   X X   X X|X 0   X 0   X 0   X X|
|  X   X X   X X   X X|X X   0 X   0 X   0 X|
|  X   X X   X X   X X|X 0   0 0   0 0   X 0|
|  0   X 0   X X   X X|X 0   0 0   0 0   0 X|
|  0   0 0   0 X   X X|0 0   0 0   0 0   0 0|
|  0   0 0   0 X   X 0|0 0   0 0   0 0   0 0|
 1 &   2 &   3 &   4 & 1 &   2 &   3 &   4 &

C                      D
|  X   0 0   X X   X X|X X   0 X   X X   X X|
|  X   0 X   0 0   X X|X X   X 0   0 X   X X|
|  X   0 0   0 X   0 X|X X   0 0   X X   X X|
|  0   0 0   0 0   X 0|X 0   0 0   0 0   X X|
|  0   0 0   0 0   0 0|0 0   0 0   0 0   0 X|
|  0   0 0   0 0   0 0|0 0   0 0   0 0   0 0|
 1 &   2 &   3 &   4 & 1 &   2 &   3 &   4 &

E
|X      ||
|X      ||
|X      ||
|X      ||
|X      ||
|X      ||
 1-2-3-4
```

Spinning prayer wheels is a form of meditation. The tune above, if played well, can also be a form of meditation. Just begin slowly and then build the speed gradually. (Pay special attention to the 1/2 count grayed note at the beginning of measures *A* and *C*.)

-Chapter 10-

This section will take you into free style playing. If you find yourself floundering, listen to the MP3s I've provided. This will give you a good feel of what this kind of playing should sound like.

-FREE-STYLE, The Holy Grail-

The Holy Grail for most flute players is to learn to play extemporaneously, (free-style). Most of the tunes we are familiar with have a definite rhythm, with the same number of beats per measure. And that gives our music a definite structure we can dance to, clap our hands to, and beat a drum to. In most cases the music we hear has four beats per measure or three beats per measure. We have listened to, and if you are a musician, played music at a steady rhythm all our lives. So it can be troublesome, at first, to throw all that predictable rhythm away and play extemporaneously. We will want to fit notes into that oh so familiar music framework that's emblazoned in our brains.

Why would we want to play extemporaneously anyway? Because playing notes as they come to us at no discernable fixed rhythm is a wonderful way to meditate. It's music straight from your heart, and it will help both you and your listeners find the meditative space that's within us all.

But I will be leading you into extemporaneous playing gradually. In the following set of tunes you will be given the notes—at first some easy notes, and later on more difficult note clusters. But I will give you only hints for the note durations. As you play through these notes you will gradually become more comfortable with the flute, and eventually you won't need anyone to give you the notes; you'll come up with your own notes on the fly. But we have to start somewhere, and these simpler tunes will make this possible for you.

-4 Magic Notes-

You've probably heard the Native American flute played in the extemporaneous free-style before. It might even be one of the reasons you bought this book. I remember the very first time I heard the beauty of this wonderful instrument. What I heard was played in the free-style, and the flute player seemed to be super human as he flew through his tune on what seemed like gossamer wings. And I remember thinking I wanted to play like that. But it took me awhile to get there. Even though the Pentatonic scale is easy to play, putting the notes together in an intelligent way wasn't obvious at first. So I began exploring the more popular side of music where the notes were familiar and so was the carefully metered out rhythms. As a long-time musician I've played in several bands, and it's fun to play with others. But one thing must be understood with free-style playing. The fact that the player plays spontaneously and with no discernable rhythm means that the player will most likely not be playing with someone else. At least they won't be playing together in a structured way. But solo playing has one very great feature: it allows the player to play his or her own heart, and that fact will bring the individual into a space that's accessible in no other way.

Special effects can add much to your free-style way of playing. It can easily be overdone if we're not careful, but when used tastefully, a well placed special effect can make a real difference. After lots of experimenting, and lots of listening to well known flute artists, I finally discovered their secrets. Special effects are used like an artist uses paint. Anyone can paint a wall an unimaginative solid color, but it requires an artist to embed picture elements into a world of light and shadow. Special effects envokes light and shadow into a tune, and you're going to learn how!

We will use just four notes in this first group of free-style chants. (Once you become comfortable playing in the free-style with just these four notes, we will fill out the rest of the Pentatonic scale.)

4 MAGIC NOTES			
X	X	X	X
X	X	X	X
X	X	X	X
X	X	X	0
X	X	0	0
X	0	0	0

IMPORTANT! **Free-style TABs do not have duration numbers.** Instead we use a free-of-duration string of notes, broken up, where appropriate, with HOLD symbols or sometimes special effect symbols. The HOLD symbols are *relative* in duration value, with the notation, "hold", being the shortest hold, and the notation, "HOLD........." being the longest hold.

The HOLD symbol from shortest to longest:

hold hold... HOLD... HOLD...... HOLD.........

You, the musician, will decide how long each HOLD should be.

Let's try some tunes in the free-style!

Wolf Whispers: Play 2x.

```
             HOLD...             HOLD...
|X X X X X----X X X X X X----||
|X X X X X----X X X X X X----||
|X X X X X----X X X X X X----||
|X X X X X----0 X X X X X----||
|X X X X X----0 X 0 X X X----||
|X 0 X X X----0 0 0 0 X X----||
```

Notice the *HOLD* notations. Play the first four notes more or less with the same note duration, but vary the durations slightly so you have room to put your emotion into each note. When you play note 5, hold that note for a few beats. Don't stop blowing the note. Blow and hold. Then play notes 6 through 10 fairly evenly and blow, then hold the last note.

Notice there is **no playing order** in this particular chant. Simply play the chant from beginning to end. Repeat it as many times as you like, and you can vary *how* you play it as well. Just have fun with it.

Notice the hyphens that follow a HOLD symbol. This is an even more visual cue to hold a blown note.

At first this way of playing might seem strange to you, but if you play each note with the idea of putting real expression into the chant, "strange" will morph into "beautiful".

Love Chant: [A]2x, [B]2x

```
A              HOLD... B                  HOLD......
|X X X X X X-----|X X X X X X X------||
|X X X X X X-----|X X X X X X X------||
|X X X X X X-----|X X X X X X X------||
|X 0 X 0 X 0-----|X 0 X X X X X------||
|X 0 0 0 0 0-----|0 0 0 X X X X------||
|X 0 0 0 0 0-----|0 0 0 0 X 0 X------||
```

As in the previous chant, play all notes fairly evenly, but then blow and hold the notes where the "HOLD" sign appears above them. As in the previous chant, play all notes somewhat evenly, but then blow and hold the notes where the "HOLD" sign appears above them. Notice the playing order. Play measure A twice, then play measure B twice. Of course, you can repeat the whole tune as often as you like.

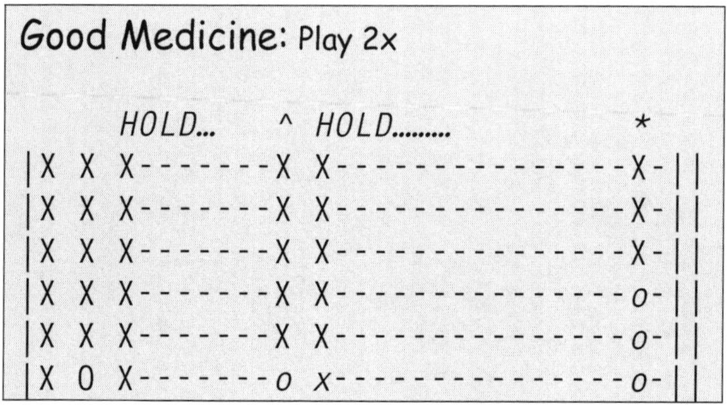

```
Good Medicine: Play 2x

      HOLD...     ^ HOLD.........             *
|X X X-------X X---------------X-||
|X X X-------X X---------------X-||
|X X X-------X X---------------X-||
|X X X-------X X---------------o-||
|X X X-------X X---------------o-||
|X 0 X-------o x---------------o-||
```

This very simple tune demonstrates the immense power of the flute. *When we blow the 3rd note, we continue to blow until the end of the entire tune, but we put in a grace note and a bark along the way while blowing this 3rd long note.* The first two notes are played without regard to specific note durations. The 3rd note is blown, then held for a time you think appropriate. While still blowing the note, quickly raise your finger on the bottom note hole, then put it back, then continue to hold the note until abruptly opening the bottom three note-holes for the bark. It's important that when you start to blow the third note, you continue to blow that note until the end of the tune. So take a big breath so you have enough air left for the bark! The grace note, (4th note), where the bottom hole is quickly opened, is quickly closed on the 5th note as the note continues to sound until you bark the last note. If this is unclear, listen to me play it on the audio files. The "bark" is explained on page 52 and the "grace" note is explained on page 54.

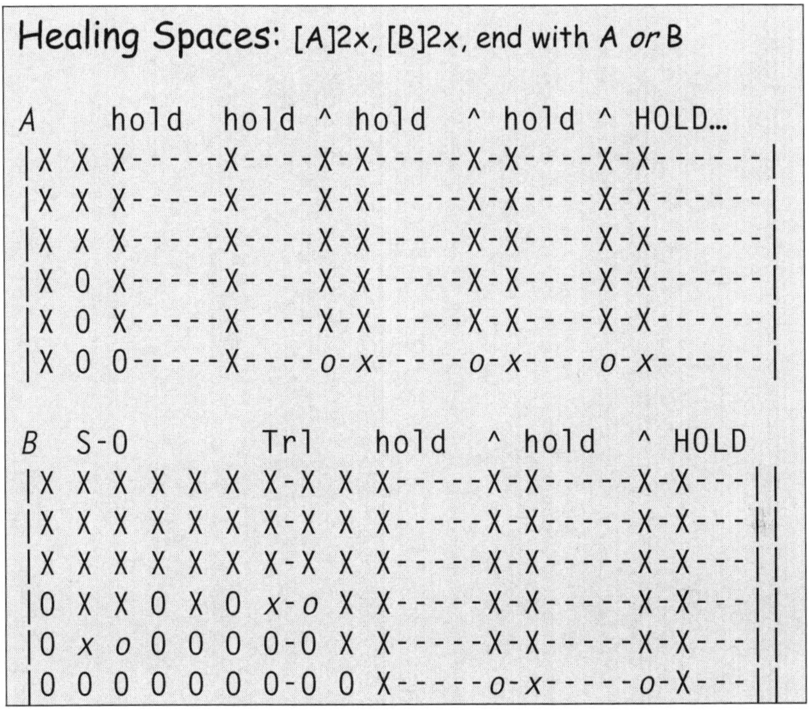

Healing Spaces: [A]2x, [B]2x, end with *A or* B

```
A     hold  hold ^ hold  ^ hold ^ HOLD...
|X X X-----X----X-X-----X-X----X-X------|
|X X X-----X----X-X-----X-X----X-X------|
|X X X-----X----X-X-----X-X----X-X------|
|X 0 X-----X----X-X-----X-X----X-X------|
|X 0 X-----X----X-X-----X-X----X-X------|
|X 0 0-----X----o-x-----o-x----o-x------|

B  S-0        Trl   hold  ^ hold  ^ HOLD
|X X X X X X X-X X X-----X-X-----X-X---||
|X X X X X X X-X X X-----X-X-----X-X---||
|X X X X X X X-X X X-----X-X-----X-X---||
|0 X X 0 X 0 x-o X X-----X-X-----X-X---||
|0 x o 0 0 0 0-0 X X-----X-X-----X-X---||
|0 0 0 0 0 0 0-0 0 X-----o-x-----o-X---||
```

There is a "slide open" from note 2 to note 3 in measure B. How to do this is covered on page 50. There is also a trill on notes 7 to 8 in measure B. (The "trill" is explained on page 48.) Also notice the grace notes in measures A and B. (The "grace" note is explained on page 54.)

Notice that the playing instructions tell you to play all of measure A twice, and then play all of measure B twice. After playing in that order, you can end by going back and playing measure A once, or you can end by playing measure B a third time. Tunes in the free-style work well when you customize. The free way of playing is very flexible to modification.

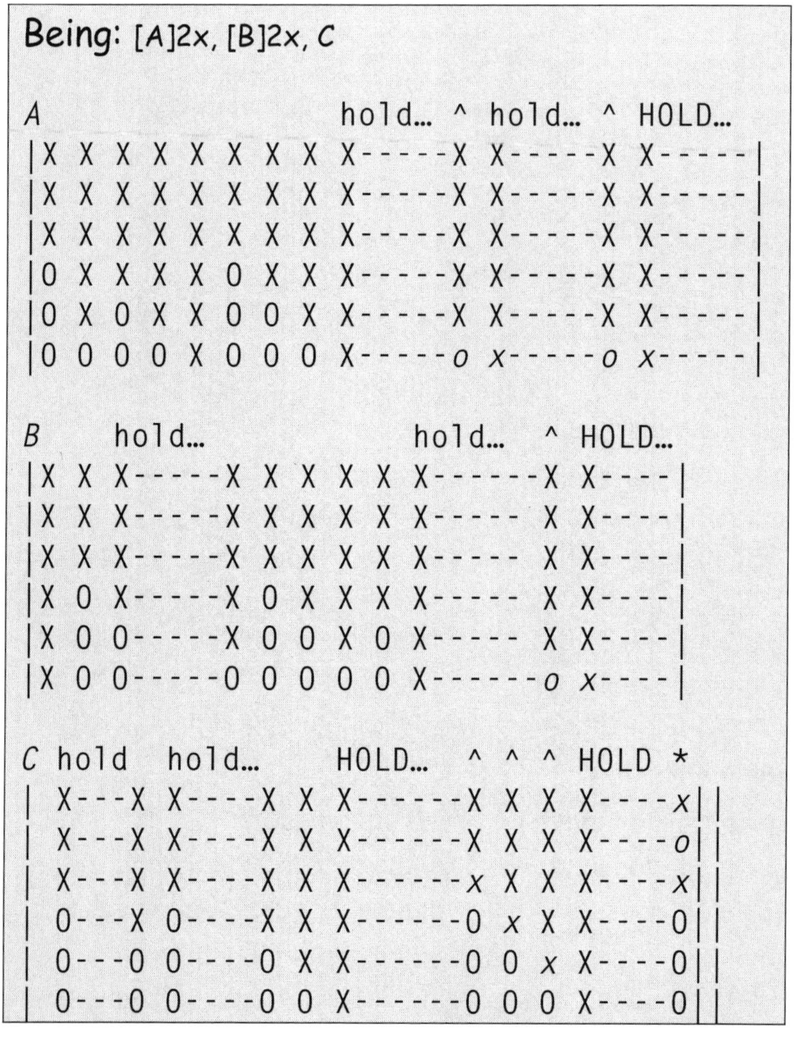

Being: [A]2x, [B]2x, C

```
A                        hold... ^ hold... ^ HOLD...
|X X X X X X X X X-----X X-----X X-----|
|X X X X X X X X X-----X X-----X X-----|
|X X X X X X X X X-----X X-----X X-----|
|0 X X X X 0 X X X-----X X-----X X-----|
|0 X 0 X X 0 0 X X-----X X-----X X-----|
|0 0 0 0 X 0 0 0 X-----o x-----o x-----|

B     hold...               hold...   ^ HOLD...
|X X X-----X X X X X X------X X----|
|X X X-----X X X X X X----- X X----|
|X X X-----X X X X X X----- X X----|
|X 0 X-----X 0 X X X X----- X X----|
|X 0 0-----X 0 0 X 0 X----- X X----|
|X 0 0-----0 0 0 0 0 X------o x----|

C hold  hold...     HOLD...   ^ ^ ^ HOLD *
| X---X X----X X X------X X X X----x||
| X---X X----X X X------X X X X----o||
| X---X X----X X X------x X X X----x||
| 0---X 0----X X X------0 x X X----0||
| 0---0 0----0 X X------0 0 x X----0||
| 0---0 0----0 0 X------0 0 0 X----0||
```

Remember, when you play note passages, you needn't do this evenly. Add emotion by lingering just a bit on some notes. In measure C notice the three grace notes, the HOLD, and the final bark. This gives us a fast and furious run to the finish. This is a simple tune to play, but as you become more comfortable with it you will find it increasingly easy to put real emotion into the simple note runs.

-Filling out the Pentatonic Scale-

The previous tunes with just four "magic" notes shows us that regardless of how many notes you might have available to you, *how* you play the notes you have yields many melodic possibilities. But now we will pay special attention to the octave and the minor 7th notes, (we needn't concern ourselves with what this means), notes that round out the Pentatonic scale. Using just another note or two can give us even more melodic possibilities. The next group of chants will illustrate this.

Grace of the Creator: [A]2x, [B]2x

```
A   HOLD... HOLD...                 HOLD.........
|X X-----X-----X X X X 0 X---------|
|X 0-----X-----X X X X X X---------|
|X X-----X-----X X X X 0 X---------|
|X 0-----0-----X X X 0 0 0---------|
|X 0-----0-----0 X 0 0 0 0---------|
|X 0-----0-----0 0 0 0 0 0---------|

B           hold... ^ HOLD......
|X X X X X-----X X---------||
|X X X X X-----X X---------||
|X X X X X-----X X---------||
|X 0 X X X-----X X---------||
|0 0 0 X X-----X X---------||
|0 0 0 0 X-----o x---------||
```

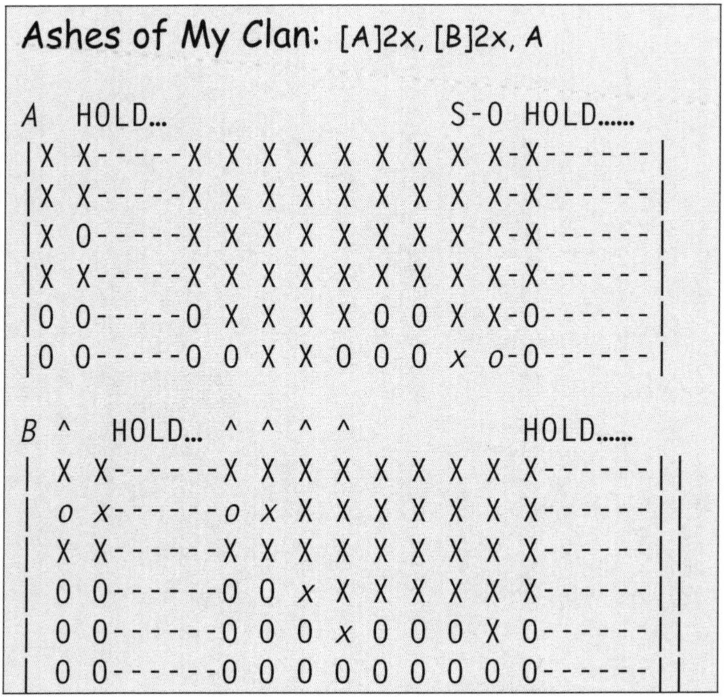

Ashes of My Clan: [A]2x, [B]2x, A

```
A   HOLD...                    S-0 HOLD......
|X  X-----X X X X X X X X X-X------|
|X  X-----X X X X X X X X X-X------|
|X  0-----X X X X X X X X X-X------|
|X  X-----X X X X X X X X X-X------|
|0  0-----0 X X X X 0 0 X X-0------|
|0  0-----0 0 X X 0 0 0 x o-0------|

B ^   HOLD... ^ ^ ^ ^               HOLD......
| X X------X X X X X X X X X------||
| o x------o x X X X X X X X------||
| X X------X X X X X X X X X------||
| 0 0------0 0 x X X X X X X------||
| 0 0------0 0 0 x 0 0 0 X 0------||
| 0 0------0 0 0 0 0 0 0 0 0------||
```

There is a grace note at the beginning of measure B. Take special notice of the four grace notes that immediately follow the first HOLD in measure B. These four grace notes will be a quick run of four notes. Notice the lower case o's and x's that indicate which note holes change from one note to another. Although these lowercase notations aren't really necessary, they will help you understand how your fingers move when going from one note to the next. You can get a better idea of how this is played from my audio recording of this tune.

Akasha (consciousness): [A]2x, B

```
A  HOLD......            HOLD... ^  HOLD...  ^ HOLD......
|X 0-------X X X X------X X------X X-----|
|X X-------X X X X------X X------X X-----|
|X 0-------X X X X------X X------X X-----|
|0 0-------0 X X X------X X------X X-----|
|0 0-------0 0 X X------X X------X-X-----|
|0 0-------0 0 0 X------o x------o x-----|

B ^ ^ ^ ^ HOLD.........          *
| 0 x X X X---------------X||
| 0 x X X X---------------0||
| x X X X X---------------X||
| 0 0 x X X---------------0||
| 0 0 0 x X---------------0||
| 0 0 0 0 X---------------0||
```

Notice the two grace notes in measure A. In measure B notice the four grace notes, then the held note under the bark symbol, finally ending with the barked note as the last note of the tune. Saying it another way, the fifth note in measure B is blown and held, and then the last note is fingered and held for just an instant, (barked). For a review, go back to the reference material where you will find many examples and a full explanation of the bark on page 52 in the reference section.

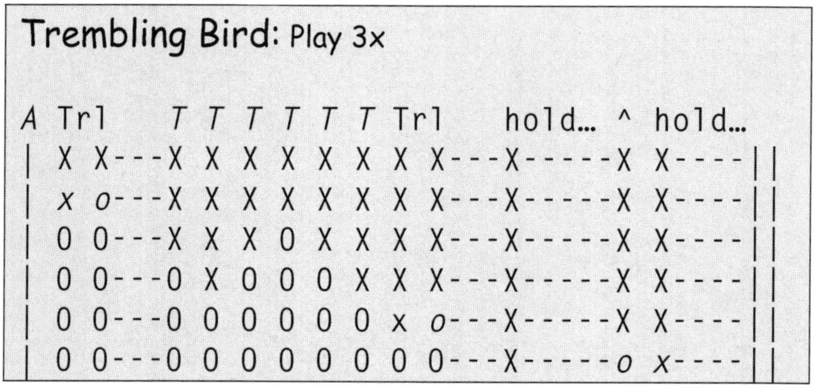

Trembling Bird: Play 3x

```
A Trl   T T T T T T Trl   hold... ^ hold...
| X X---X X X X X X X X---X-----X X----||
| x o---X X X X X X X X---X-----X X----||
| 0 0---X X X 0 X X X X---X-----X X----||
| 0 0---0 X 0 0 0 X X X---X-----X X----||
| 0 0---0 0 0 0 0 0 x o---X-----X X----||
| 0 0---0 0 0 0 0 0 0 0---X-----o x----||
```

The **trill** is a nice effect, but it can be overdone so should be used sparingly. I used it to excess here to demonstrate how it can help paint the picture of the tune. I named the tune "Trembling Bird" because the trill delivers a pleasant warbling sound, much like a song bird might sound in your back yard.

Notice the sharply tongued notes as indicated by the *"T"*. Birds don't walk smoothly. They move herky jerky. So when you play the individual notes, sharply tonguing them will give this effect.

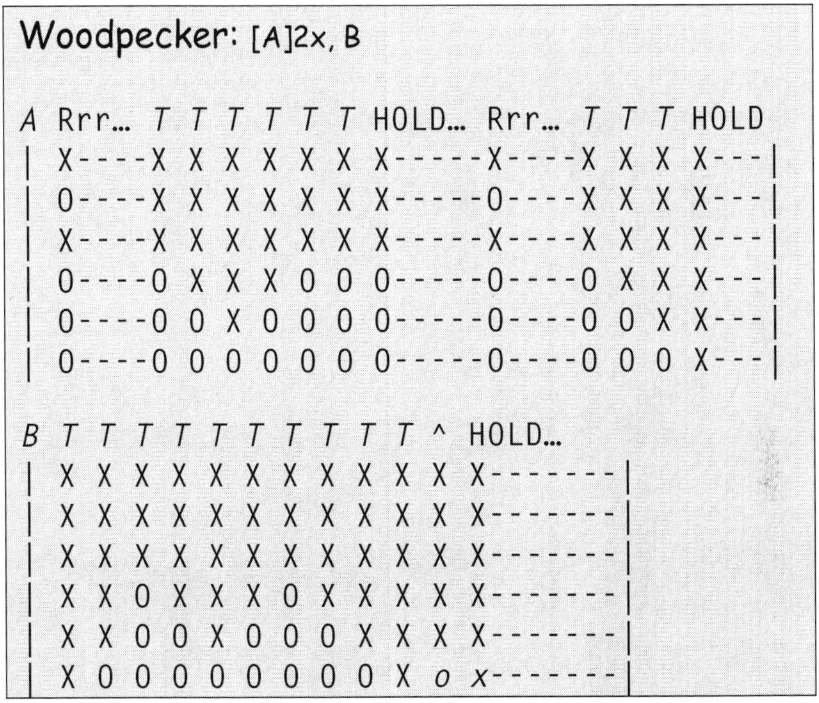

```
Woodpecker: [A]2x, B

A Rrr… T T T T T T HOLD… Rrr… T T T HOLD
| X----X X X X X X X-----X----X X X X---|
| O----X X X X X X X-----O----X X X X---|
| X----X X X X X X X-----X----X X X X---|
| O----O X X X O O O-----O----O X X X---|
| O----O O X O O O O-----O----O O X X---|
| O----O O O O O O O-----O----O O O X---|

B T T T T T T T T T T ^ HOLD…
| X X X X X X X X X X X X-------|
| X X X X X X X X X X X X-------|
| X X X X X X X X X X X X-------|
| X X O X X X O X X X X X-------|
| X X O O X O O O X X X X-------|
| X O O O O O O O O X o x-------|
```

The raspberry effect is used in this tune. You can read about this effect on page 49. The symbol, "Rrr" is used to show which notes to apply the effect to. The raspberry on the last note in measure B is held longer than those in measure A, giving this tune a novel ending.

As you play this tune, imagine a woodpecker rat-a-ta-tatting for awhile, then dancing around on the branch in that stilted way birds do. As you play those notes not connected to each other with the hyphen, tongue each note sharply. (This is what the *"T"*, symbol tells you to do.) Birds don't move smoothly. They move with a quick, stilted motion. Express this in your playing. Hear me play this on the audio files that accompany this book.

-Chapter 11-

7 Daily Extemporaneous Chants

The following seven chants are fairly short. They are ideas you can play and add to as you see fit. Follow your muse as you meditate while you play them. Add new notes, subtract notes, add effects wherever you like.

Each chant can be repeated as many times as you like.

Stealthy Lion (Monday): 2x

```
A S-0 S-C                               hold   ^  *
| X X X X X X X X X X X X X X X----X X||
| X X o x X X X X X X 0 X X X X----X X||
| X X X X X X X X X X X X X X X----X X||
| x o 0 0 X X X X X 0 0 0 X X X----X X||
| 0 0 0 0 0 X X X 0 0 0 0 0 X X----X X||
| 0 0 0 0 0 0 X 0 0 0 0 0 0 0 X----o x||
```

Pay very close attention to those note-hole numbers under the slide symbols that are in *italics.* These holes are the ones you slide off of and onto.

Sleeping Child (Tuesday): 2x

```
A     hold...           hold...           HOLD.........
|X X X-----X X X X-----X X X X------||
|X X 0-----X X X X-----X X X X------||
|X X X-----X X X X-----X X X X------||
|X X 0-----0 X X X-----X X X X------||
|X 0 0-----0 0 X 0-----X X X X------||
|0 0 0-----0 0 0 0-----0 X 0 X------||
```

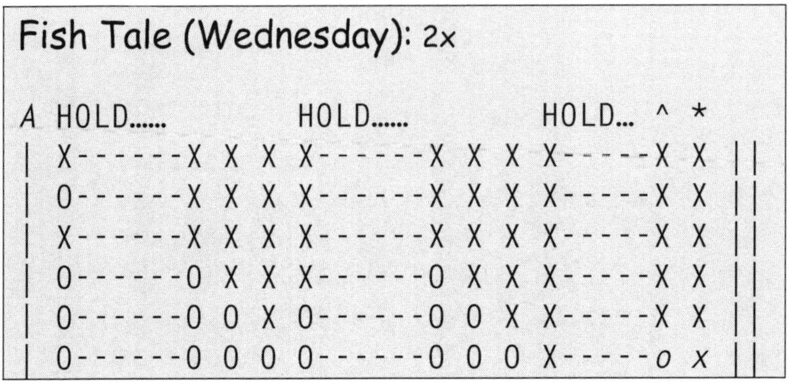

Fish Tale (Wednesday): 2x

```
A HOLD......        HOLD......        HOLD... ^ *
| X------X X X X------X X X X-----X X ||
| 0------X X X X------X X X X-----X X ||
| X------X X X X------X X X X-----X X ||
| 0------0 X X X------0 X X X-----X X ||
| 0------0 0 X 0------0 0 X X-----X X ||
| 0------0 0 0 0------0 0 0 X-----o x ||
```

The last two notes in this chant is a combination of a grace note and a bark. The grace note is held for only an instant, but the note under the *, like a bark, is blown rather forcefully then *closed* quickly. The last two notes, then, are played quickly in succession, almost like slamming a door.

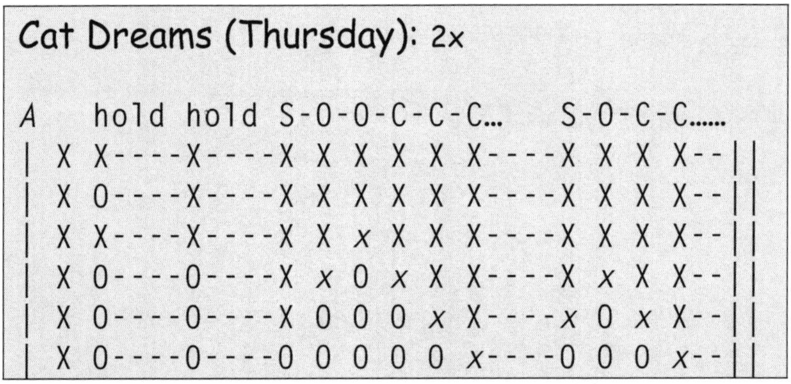

Cat Dreams (Thursday): 2x

```
A   hold hold S-0-0-C-C-C...   S-0-C-C......
| X X----X----X X X X X X----X X X X--||
| X 0----X----X X X X X X----X X X X--||
| X X----X----X X x X X X----X X X X--||
| X 0----0----X x 0 x X X----X x X X--||
| X 0----0----X 0 0 0 x X----x 0 x X--||
| X 0----0----0 0 0 0 0 x----0 0 0 x--||
```

Notice the slide-open and slide-close symbols. They are combined because we slide open and then slide closed within a run of notes. The lowercase note-holes in italics will help you track which notes are opened and closed. It helps to pause a bit between slides. Think of how fluid a cat moves as you do the slides.

Rascally Rabbit (Friday): 2x

```
A       hold         hold              HOLD *
|X X X X---X X X X---X X X X X X----x||
|X X X X---X X X X---X X X X X X----o||
|X X X X---X X X X---X X X X X X----x||
|X O X O---X O X O---X X O X X X----O||
|X O O O---X O O O---X X O O X X----O||
|X O O O---X O O O---X O O O O X----O||
```

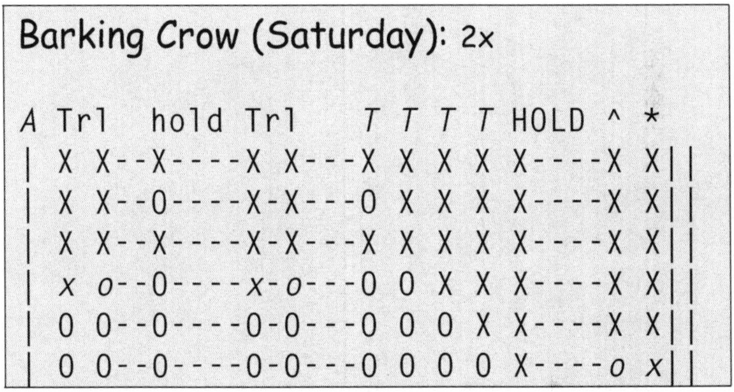

Barking Crow (Saturday): 2x

```
A Trl  hold Trl    T T T T HOLD ^ *
| X X--X----X X---X X X X X----X X||
| X X--O----X-X---O X X X X----X X||
| X X--X----X-X---X X X X X----X X||
| x o--O----x-o---O O X X X----X X||
| O O--O----O-O---O O O X X----X X||
| O O--O----O-O---O O O O X----o x||
```

The "Barking Crow" chant uses a combination of effects. When you end the trill, hold for just a bit and then quickly follow with the next note. (Notice the *x* and *o* in italics in the notes that are trilled. Rapidly open and close this note hole to make the "Trl" effect.)

Notice the four sharply tongued notes just before the last HOLD.

The last two notes are a combination of a grace note and a bark. The effect is like two rapidly played notes in succession.

The grace note and bark is a commonly used device when playing extemporaneously. They fit well when you want to put a "button" on the end of a tune.

Strutting Crane (Sunday): 2x

```
A^ HOLD T T T T T ^ hold ^ ^ ^ ^ *
|X X----X X X X X o X----o x X X X||
|X O----X X X X X o X----o x X X X||
|X X----X X X X X X X----X X X X X||
|X O----O X X X O O O----O O x X X||
|X O----O X X O O O O----O O O x X||
|X O----O X O O O O O----O O O O x||
```

The first note is a grace note, but the ^ symbol is almost hidden as it's tucked just behind the 'A'. The timing on this tune is a bit tricky. If you're puzzled, listen to me play it on the audio files that came with this book.

-Chapter 12-

Wakan Tanka

Traditional Songs of the Early Native American

It has proven to be quite difficult to find original Native American flute tunes. That's because passing down tunes through generations has been in the oral tradition, not the written tradition. It's been only very recently that we've begun using tablature to record the traditional tunes so others can play them. But there are a few Native American flute players that have successfully tracked down traditional tunes from very old field recordings made back in the early 20th Century. If you are interested in early Native American music, check out **Smithsonian Folkways** for CDs and downloads. Unfortunately the Smithsonian doesn't have an easy URL to type in. So to find their site, type "Smithsonian Folkways" into any search engine and it will give you a link that will take you to the Folkways home page.

Corn Grinding Song: [A]2x, [B-C]2x, [D]

```
A             HOLD......            hold... HOLD......
|X X X X X O------X O X X X-----X------|
|X O O O O X------O X O X X-----X------|
|X X X X X O------X O X X X-----X------|
|X O O O O O------O O O O X-----X------|
|X O O O O O------O O O O O-----O------|
|X O O O O O------O O O O O-----O------|

B          hold  HOLD... C         hold... HOLD...
|X X X X X-----X-----|X X X X-----X----|
|X X X X X-----X-----|X X X X-----X----|
|X X X X X-----X-----|X X X X-----X----|
|X O X X X-----X-----|X X X X-----X----|
|O O O X X-----X-----|X X X X-----X----|
|O O O O X-----X-----|X O X X-----X----|

D      hold...                  hold ^ hold *
|X X X X-----X X X X X X X----X X----X||
|X X X X-----X X X X X X X----X X----o||
|X X X X-----X X X X X X X----X X----X||
|X X X O-----X X X X X X X----X X----o||
|X X O O-----O X O X O X X----X X----o||
|X O O O-----O O O O O O X----o x----o||
```

This traditional tune is beautifully played by **R. Carlos Nakai**, a Lakota Sioux flute artist, and the man who arguably reignited everyone's interest in the Native American flute. Without his efforts, the Native American flute wouldn't be nearly as popular as it is today. Nakai earned his Masters in classical trumpet, but soon after graduating, he began playing a Native American flute a friend had given him. Lucky for us all, we have a real mentor for the rest of us. (Nakai's many albums are available on iTunes.)

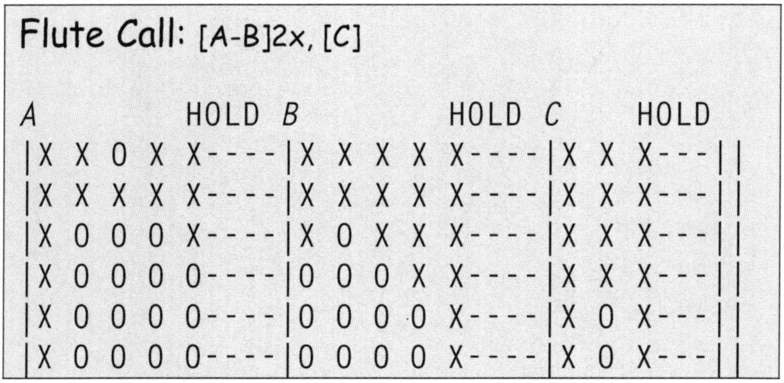

```
Flute Call: [A-B]2x, [C]

A         HOLD B           HOLD C      HOLD
|X X O X X----|X X X X X----|X X X---||
|X X X X X----|X X X X X----|X X X---||
|X O O O X----|X O X X X----|X X X---||
|X O O O O----|O O O X X----|X X X---||
|X O O O O----|O O O O X----|X O X---||
|X O O O O----|O O O O X----|X O X---||
```

Doc Tate Nevaquaya played this traditional tune. Doc was a self-taught artist, Native American flute player of the Comanche tribe, composer, dancer, lecturer, and Methodist lay minister. Before R. Carlos Nakai made the flute popular with everyone, Doc Tate gently introduced us to it. Doc made his first album of the Native American flute in 1973. The above tune is one of the prettier traditional tunes Doc played.

Doc's album is available on iTunes, should you be interested.

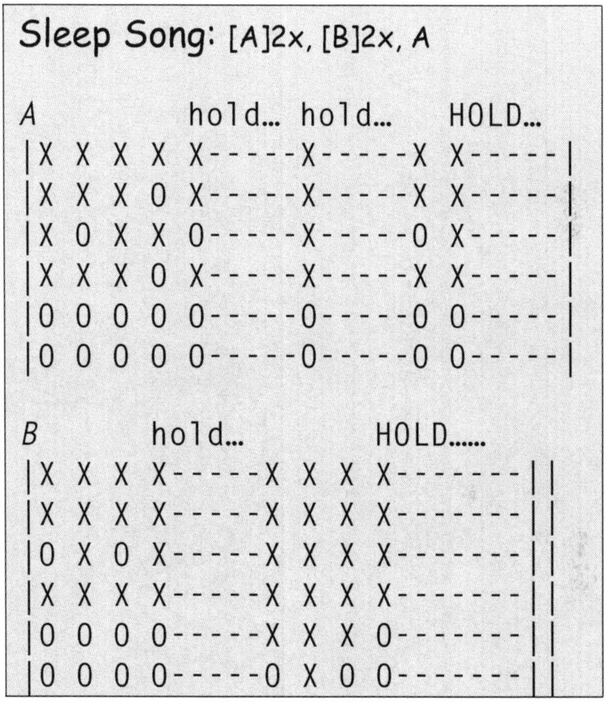

Sleep Song: [A]2x, [B]2x, A

```
A          hold... hold...    HOLD...
|X X X X X-----X-----X X-----|
|X X X O X-----X-----X X-----|
|X O X X O-----X-----O X-----|
|X X X O X-----X-----X X-----|
|O O O O O-----O-----O O-----|
|O O O O O-----O-----O O-----|

B        hold...         HOLD......
|X X X X-----X X X X-------||
|X X X X-----X X X X-------||
|O X O X-----X X X X-------||
|X X X X-----X X X X-------||
|O O O O-----X X X O-------||
|O O O O-----O X O O-------||
```

This traditional tune was played by Doc Tate Nevaquaya. I think of this pensive tune as a lullaby.

Zuni Song: [A, B]2x, C

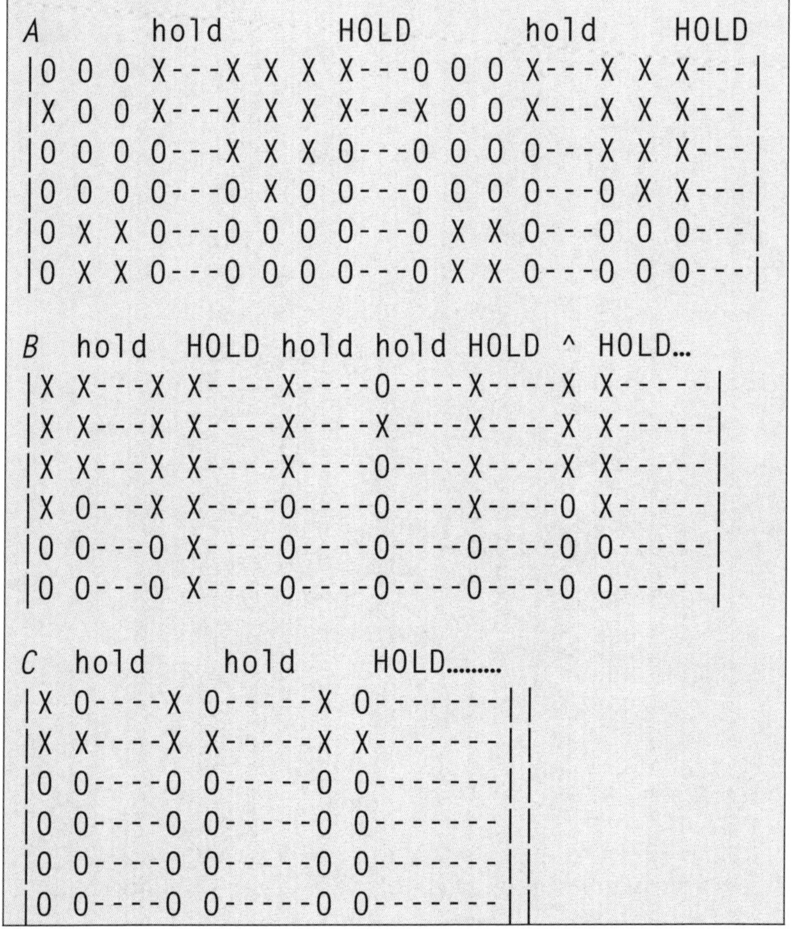

```
A        hold         HOLD          hold     HOLD
|0 0 0 X---X X X X---0 0 0 X---X X X---|
|X 0 0 X---X X X X---X 0 0 X---X X X---|
|0 0 0 0---X X X 0---0 0 0 0---X X X---|
|0 0 0 0---0 X 0 0---0 0 0 0---0 X X---|
|0 X X 0---0 0 0 0---0 X X 0---0 0 0---|
|0 X X 0---0 0 0 0---0 X X 0---0 0 0---|

B  hold  HOLD hold hold HOLD ^ HOLD...
|X X---X X----X----0----X----X X-----|
|X X---X X----X----X----X----X X-----|
|X X---X X----X----0----X----X X-----|
|X 0---X X----0----0----X----0 X-----|
|0 0---0 X----0----0----0----0 0-----|
|0 0---0 X----0----0----0----0 0-----|

C  hold     hold     HOLD.........
|X 0----X 0-----X 0-------||
|X X----X X-----X X-------||
|0 0----0 0-----0 0-------||
|0 0----0 0-----0 0-------||
|0 0----0 0-----0 0-------||
|0 0----0 0-----0 0-------||
```

This haunting traditional tune is in the repertoire of R. Carlos Nakai. Nakai has recorded many albums, including several albums with his jazz quartet and several with standard transverse flute jazz legend, Paul Horn.

-Chapter 13-

BONUS Tunes

This last section of tunes covers lots of ground. Some of the tunes are quite challenging. Be sure to listen to my interpretation of the tunes on the included audio files with this book.

IMPORTANT: These bonus tunes are a mix of tunes with a strict rhythm like those tunes we studied in the beginning of the book, and extemporaneous tunes which we studied in the last part of the book. If you see note duration numbers below the notes, you know to follow the beat. If there are no numbers, the tune is extemporaneous and should be interpreted in your own way, using the HOLD symbols as guides where called for.

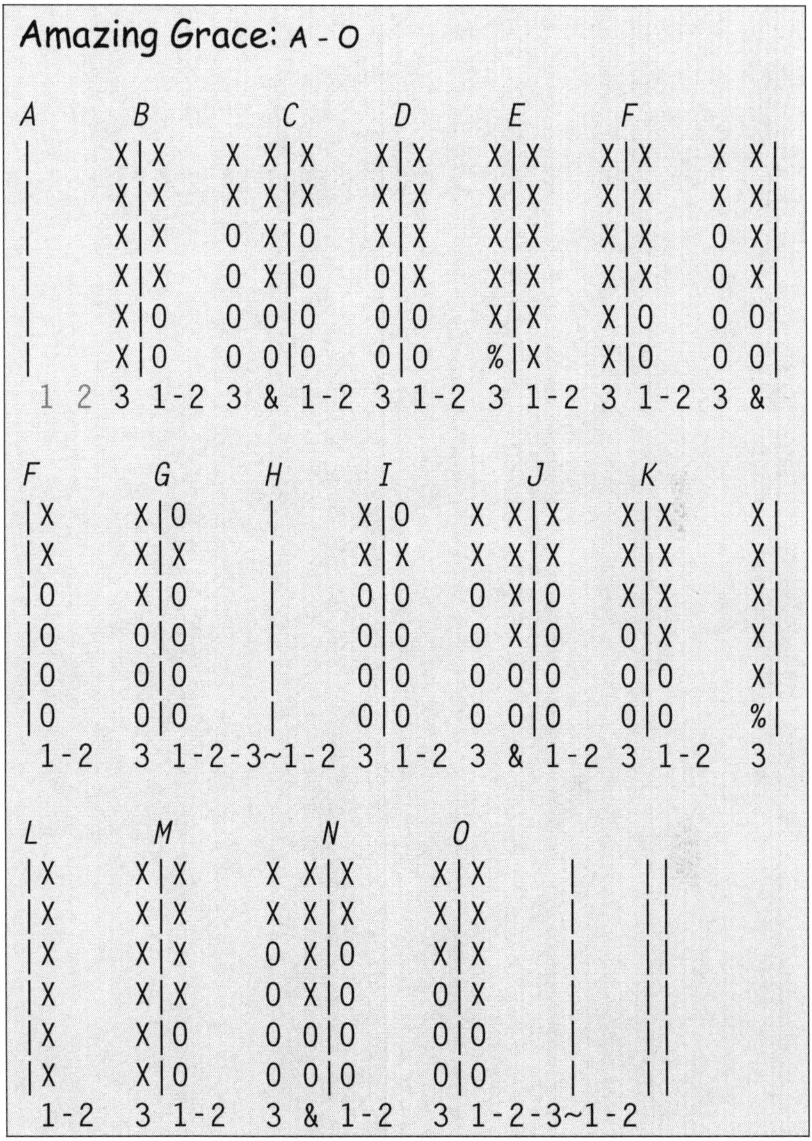

Amazing Grace: A - O

```
A     B       C     D     E     F
|    X|X   X X|X   X|X   X|X   X|X   X X|
|    X|X   X X|X   X|X   X|X   X|X   X X|
|    X|X   0 X|0   X|X   X|X   X|X   0 X|
|    X|X   0 X|0   0|X   X|X   X|X   0 X|
|    X|0   0 0|0   0|0   X|X   X|0   0 0|
|    X|0   0 0|0   0|0   %|X   X|0   0 0|
 1 2 3 1-2 3 & 1-2 3 1-2 3 1-2 3 1-2 3 &

F      G     H     I       J     K
|X    X|0    |    X|0   X X|X   X|X    X|
|X    X|X    |    X|X   X X|X   X|X    X|
|0    X|0    |    0|0   0 X|0   X|X    X|
|0    0|0    |    0|0   0 X|0   0|X    X|
|0    0|0    |    0|0   0 0|0   0|0    X|
|0    0|0    |    0|0   0 0|0   0|0    %|
 1-2  3 1-2-3~1-2 3 1-2 3 & 1-2 3 1-2  3

L      M        N      O
|X    X|X    X X|X    X|X    |   ||
|X    X|X    X X|X    X|X    |   ||
|X    X|X    0 X|0    X|X    |   ||
|X    X|X    0 X|0    0|X    |   ||
|X    X|0    0 0|0    0|0    |   ||
|X    X|0    0 0|0    0|0    |   ||
 1-2  3 1-2  3 & 1-2  3 1-2-3~1-2
```

Notice the half-hole, **(%)** notes in measures D and K. This is the half-hole note as discussed on page 36. We could not correctly play the melody without half-holing the bottom note hole. Be sure to listen to Chris Fuqua's version of

Amazing Grace. The name of Chris's version is p159-Cshrp_AmazingGrace-Fuqua.mp3.

WAYFARIN' STRANGER IS THE PERFECT TUNE TO PLAY WITHIN THE PENTATONIC SCALE: Many folk tunes, regardless of country or region, have a soulful sound. "Wayfarin' Stranger" is one of those tunes. And it fits perfectly within the standard Pentatonic scale (plus the octave note). When you begin playing this tune, you'll probably recognize it. This tune is not in the free-style. It has a definite rhythm of 4b/m. But it's a beautiful piece to meditate by, and that's why I include it in this book.

Pay close attention to the playing order of the measures. If you don't follow it, the song won't make any sense.

Turn the page for the 2-page tablature of Wayfarin' Stranger. →

Wayfarin' Stranger: [A-I], [B-E], [J-U], [B-E], [J-L]

```
A       B       C       D       E
|  X X X|X      |  X X X|X X    |  X X X|
|  X X X|X      |  X X X|X X    |  X X X|
|  X X X|X      |  X X X|X X    |  X X X|
|  X X 0|0      |  X 0 X|X X    |  X X 0|
|  X X 0|0      |  0 0 0|X X    |  X X 0|
|  X X 0|0      |  0 0 0|0 X    |  X X 0|
 1 2 3 4 1-2-3-4~1 2 3 4 1 2-3-4~1 2 3 4

F       G       H       I       J
|X      |  X X X|X      |  X X X|X       |
|X      |  X X X|X      |  X X X|X       |
|X      |  X X X|X      |  X X X|X       |
|X      |  X X X|0      |  X X X|X       |
|0      |  X X 0|0      |  X X 0|0       |
|0      |  X 0 0|0      |  X X 0|0       |
 1-2-3-4~1 2 3 4 1-2-3-4~1 2 3 4 1-2-3-4~

K       L       M       N       O
|  X X X|X      |  X X X|0      |  X 0 X|
|  X X X|X      |  X X 0|X      |  0 X 0|
|  X X X|X      |  X X X|0      |  X 0 X|
|  X X X|X      |  0 0 0|0      |  0 0 0|
|  X X X|X      |  0 0 0|0      |  0 0 0|
|  0 X 0|X      |  0 0 0|0      |  0 0 0|
 1 2 3 4 1-2-3-4~1 2 3 4 1-2-3-4~1 2 3 4
```

CONTINUED ON NEXT PAGE→

```
Wayfarin' Stranger CONTINUED....

P         Q         R         S         T
|X X      |  X X X|0          |  X X X|X          |
|X X      |  X X 0|X          |  0 X X|X          |
|X X      |  X X X|0          |  X X X|X          |
|0 X      |  0 0 0|0          |  0 0 X|X          |
|0 X      |  0 0 0|0          |  0 0 X|0          |
|0 0      |  0 0 0|0          |  0 0 0|0          |
 1 2-3-4~1 2 3 4 1-2-3-4~1 2 3 4 1-2-3-4~

U
|  X X X|
|  X X X|
|  X X X|
|  X X 0|
|  X X 0|
|  X X 0|
 1 2 3 4
```

NOTE: This venerable old tune isn't difficult to play, but the pathway through it might call for penciling in some arrows so it's easier to follow the path of the playing order of each measure.

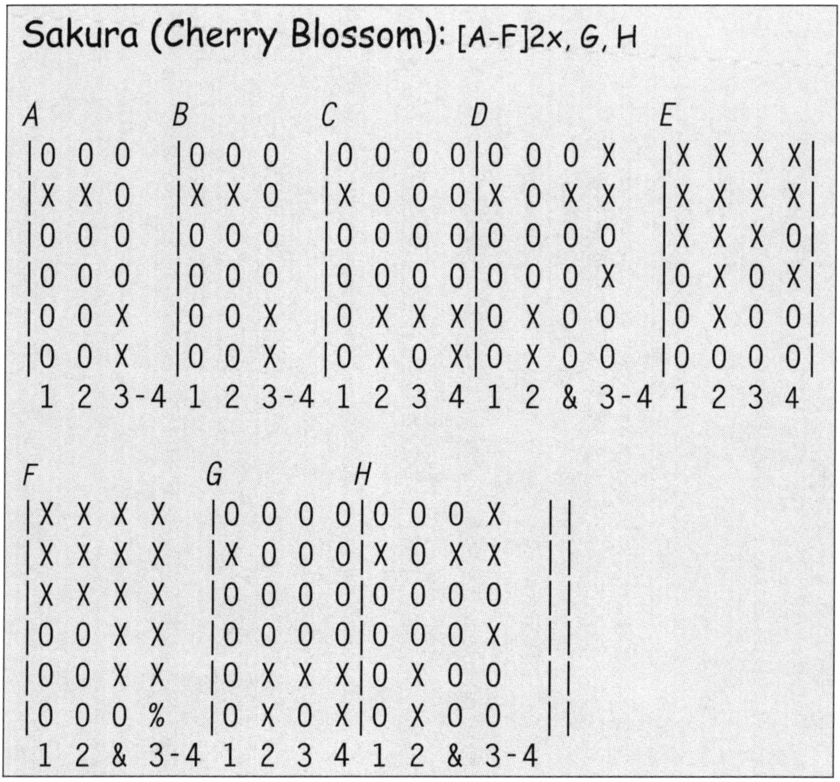

Sakura (Cherry Blossom): [A-F]2x, G, H

```
A       B       C       D             E
|0 0 0  |0 0 0  |0 0 0 0|0 0 0 X     |X X X X|
|X X 0  |X X 0  |X 0 0 0|X 0 X X     |X X X X|
|0 0 0  |0 0 0  |0 0 0 0|0 0 0 0     |X X X 0|
|0 0 0  |0 0 0  |0 0 0 0|0 0 0 X     |0 X 0 X|
|0 0 X  |0 0 X  |0 X X X|0 X 0 0     |0 X 0 0|
|0 0 X  |0 0 X  |0 X 0 X|0 X 0 0     |0 0 0 0|
 1 2 3-4 1 2 3-4 1 2 3 4 1 2 & 3-4 1 2 3 4

F          G       H
|X X X X   |0 0 0 0|0 0 0 X   ||
|X X X X   |X 0 0 0|X 0 X X   ||
|X X X X   |0 0 0 0|0 0 0 0   ||
|0 0 X X   |0 0 0 0|0 0 0 X   ||
|0 0 X X   |0 X X X|0 X 0 0   ||
|0 0 0 %   |0 X 0 X|0 X 0 0   ||
 1 2 & 3-4 1 2 3 4 1 2 & 3-4
```

This is a fun tune because you can make your Native American flute sound much like the Japanese bamboo endblown flute. Once you learn the tune and become comfortable with it, it will probably be one of your favorite tunes for meditation. The note duration numbers tell us the tune has a strict beat. Note the half-hole, **(%)**, note in measure F.

Introitus - Adorate Deum: [A, B, C]2x

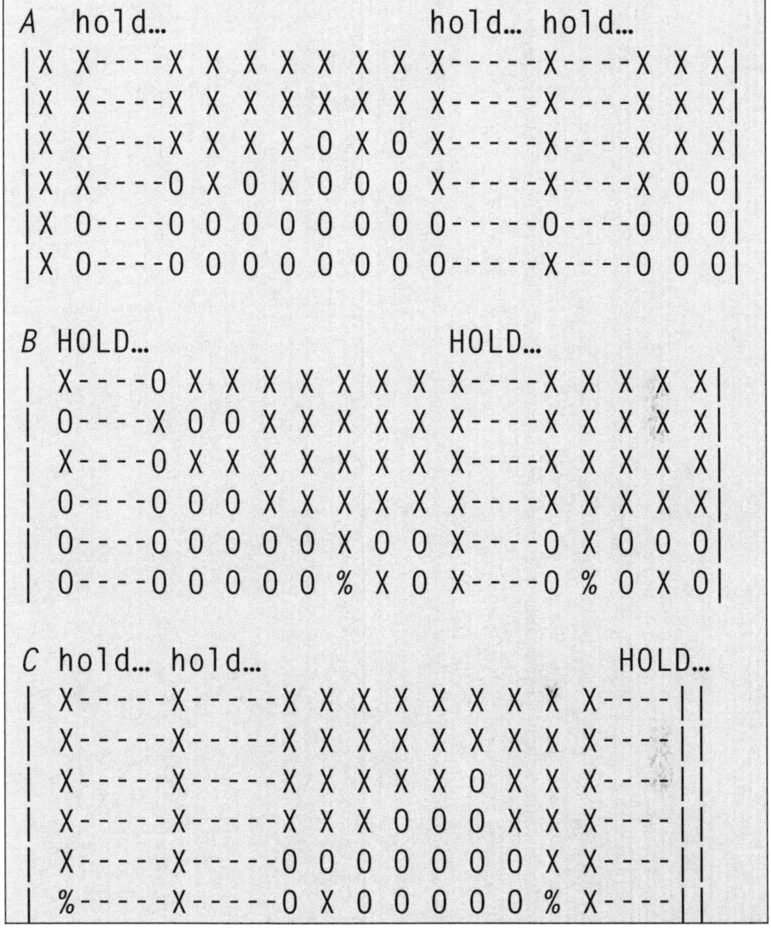

```
A  hold...                 hold... hold...
|X X----X X X X X X X X-----X----X X X|
|X X----X X X X X X X X-----X----X X X|
|X X----X X X X 0 X 0 X-----X----X X X|
|X X----0 X 0 X 0 0 0 X-----X----X 0 0|
|X 0----0 0 0 0 0 0 0 0-----0----0 0 0|
|X 0----0 0 0 0 0 0 0 0-----X----0 0 0|

B HOLD...                   HOLD...
| X----0 X X X X X X X X----X X X X X|
| 0----X 0 0 X X X X X X----X X X X X|
| X----0 X X X X X X X X----X X X X X|
| 0----0 0 0 X X X X X X----X X X X X|
| 0----0 0 0 0 0 X 0 0 X----0 X 0 0 0|
| 0----0 0 0 0 0 % X 0 X----0 % 0 X 0|

C hold... hold...                  HOLD...
| X-----X-----X X X X X X X X X----||
| X-----X-----X X X X X X X X X----||
| X-----X-----X X X X X 0 X X X----||
| X-----X-----X X X 0 0 0 X X X----||
| X-----X-----0 0 0 0 0 0 0 X X----||
| %-----X-----0 X 0 0 0 0 0 % X----||
```

Gregorian chants are serene, but they can be difficult to reproduce on an instrument. Traditionally, the chants are sung with an "Ooooo" sound in unison by several monks. The scale is very interesting. It's kind of a mix of minor and major. The above chant is easy to play but difficult to play well. Notice the (%) half-hole notes in measures B and C. This chant, as in all Grogorian chants, has no discernable rhythm and is played in a flowing way. Blow smoothly. Tongue only when necessary.

Jewish Folk Tune: [A-D]2x, [E-F]2x, G, H

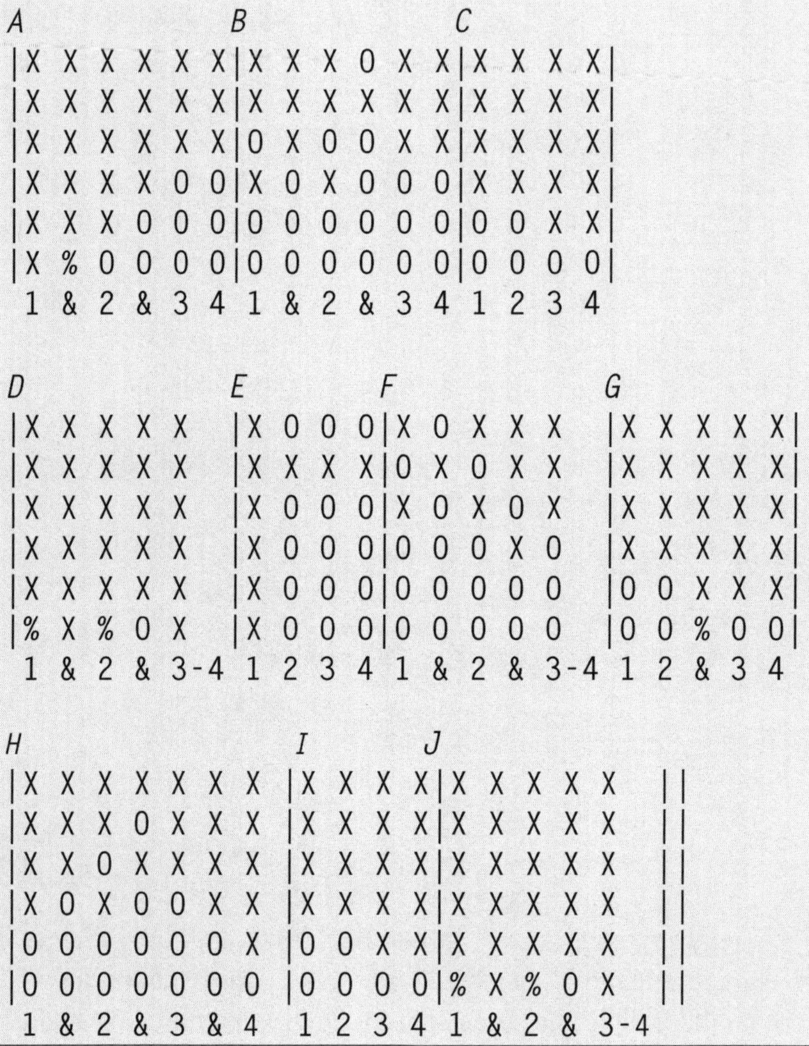

```
A           B           C
|X X X X X X|X X X 0 X X|X X X X|
|X X X X X X|X X X X X X|X X X X|
|X X X X X X|0 X 0 0 X X|X X X X|
|X X X X 0 0|X 0 X 0 0 0|X X X X|
|X X X 0 0 0|0 0 0 0 0 0|0 0 X X|
|X % 0 0 0 0|0 0 0 0 0 0|0 0 0 0|
 1 & 2 & 3 4 1 & 2 & 3 4 1 2 3 4
```

```
D           E       F           G
|X X X X X  |X 0 0 0|X 0 X X X  |X X X X X|
|X X X X X  |X X X X|0 X 0 X X  |X X X X X|
|X X X X X  |X 0 0 0|X 0 X 0 X  |X X X X X|
|X X X X X  |X 0 0 0|0 0 0 X 0  |X X X X X|
|X X X X X  |X 0 0 0|0 0 0 0 0  |0 0 X X X|
|% X % 0 X  |X 0 0 0|0 0 0 0 0  |0 0 % 0 0|
 1 & 2 & 3-4 1 2 3 4 1 & 2 & 3-4 1 2 & 3 4
```

```
H             I       J
|X X X X X X X |X X X X|X X X X X   ||
|X X X 0 X X X |X X X X|X X X X X   ||
|X X 0 X X X X |X X X X|X X X X X   ||
|X 0 X 0 0 X X |X X X X|X X X X X   ||
|0 0 0 0 0 0 X |0 0 X X|X X X X X   ||
|0 0 0 0 0 0 0 |0 0 0 0|% X % 0 X   ||
 1 & 2 & 3 & 4  1 2 3 4 1 & 2 & 3-4
```

Pay careful attention to the playing order. Notice the note duration numbers that give this tune a strict beat. Also notice the half-hole, (**%**), notes in measures A, D, G, and J.

Asato Maa:

Intro, A-C, D-E, B-C, [B-C, D-E, B-C]2x, Intro to end

INTRO: Start with all holes closed, blow and hold, then slowly slide open the bottom two holes.

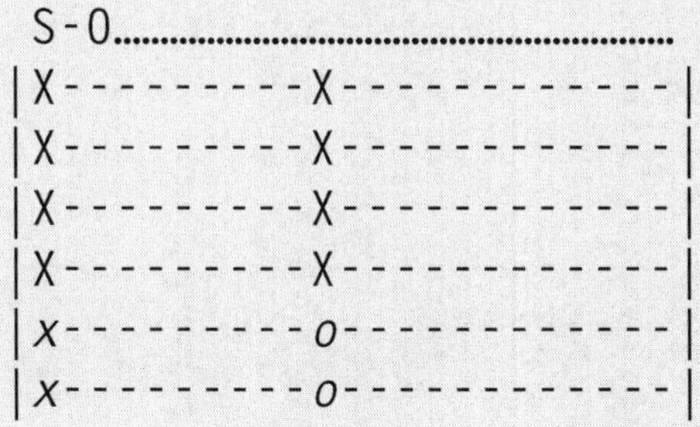

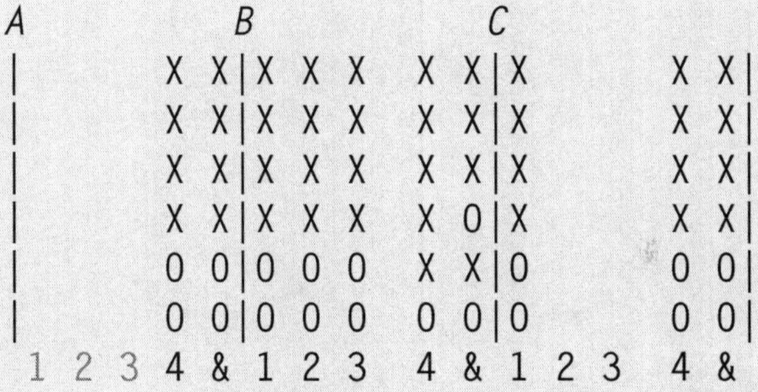

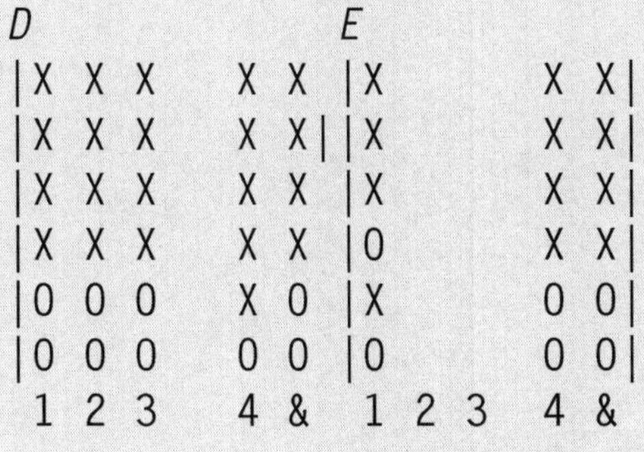

```
 S-0.............................
|X---------X-----------|
|X---------X-----------|
|X---------X-----------|
|X---------X-----------|
|x---------o-----------|
|x---------o-----------|

A            B          C
|      X X|X X X  X X|X      X X|
|      X X|X X X  X X|X      X X|
|      X X|X X X  X X|X      X X|
|      X X|X X X  X 0|X      X X|
|      0 0|0 0 0  X X|0      0 0|
|      0 0|0 0 0  0 0|0      0 0|
 1 2 3 4 & 1 2 3  4 & 1 2 3  4 &

D          E
|X X X    X X |X     X X|
|X X X    X X||X     X X|
|X X X    X X |X     X X|
|X X X    X X |0     X X|
|0 0 0    X 0 |X     0 0|
|0 0 0    0 0 |0     0 0|
 1 2 3    4 &  1 2 3 4 &
```

This ancient Hindu chant is great fun to play. You can play it over and over, just like a mantra.

Taps: A - H

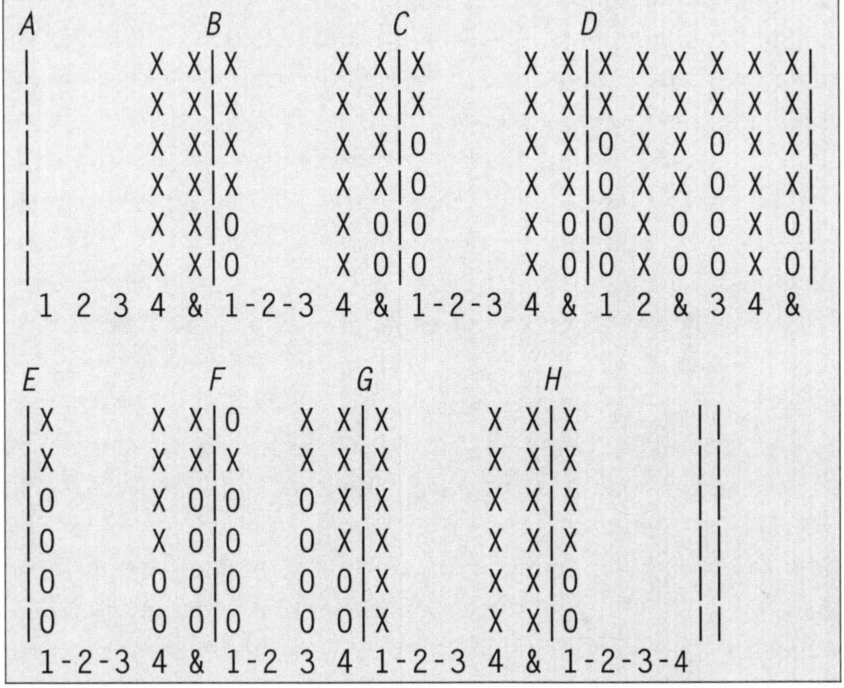

```
A         B         C         D
|      X X|X     X X|X     X X|X X X X X X|
|      X X|X     X X|X     X X|X X X X X X|
|      X X|X     X X|0     X X|0 X X 0 X X|
|      X X|X     X X|0     X X|0 X X 0 X X|
|      X X|0     X 0|0     X 0|0 X 0 0 X 0|
|      X X|0     X 0|0     X 0|0 X 0 0 X 0|
 1 2 3 4 & 1-2-3 4 & 1-2-3 4 & 1 2 & 3 4 &

E         F       G         H
|X     X X|0   X X|X     X X|X      ||
|X     X X|X   X X|X     X X|X      ||
|0     X 0|0   0 X|X     X X|X      ||
|0     X 0|0   0 X|X     X X|X      ||
|0     0 0|0   0 0|X     X X|0      ||
|0     0 0|0   0 0|X     X X|0      ||
 1-2-3 4 & 1-2 3 4 1-2-3 4 & 1-2-3-4
```

ORIGIN: The tune, TAPS, is very familiar to all Americans. It's the bugle call played at graveside during military funerals. It's also played at every annual Memorial Day ceremony all across America. Traditionally, TAPS is played close to or amid those gathered for the memorial ceremony. When the bugle call ends, the tune is played again, this time by a bugle some distance away. This adds an ethereal echo to the first call. You might try playing this along with yourself and a friend who also plays the Native American flute. Just be sure that both flutes are in the same key!

-Symmetry-

SYMMETRY: An important principle when playing extemporaneously is that of **symmetry**. This technique allows us to play the flute *truly* extemporaneously. There is no tablature. We simply pick up our flute and play. It's always good, especially if you are new at this, to make the first note all holes closed. Simply begin playing any group of notes **within the Pentatonic scale**. Then repeat the phrase you just played. Then we play a different phrase, and then repeat what we just played. Repeating a phrase gives our tune a sense of balance, of symmetry. For true symmetry we would play each phrase an even number of times, (usually just twice). Then we would go on with the next phrase and repeat it. Of course, you can repeat a phrase as many times as you like, or not repeat a phrase at all. You might repeat some phrases and not others. But if you play a phrase an even number of times, most of the time, the tune will sound like you have been playing the Native American flute all your life. And this symmetry, this sense of balance, increases the power of your tune. I have recorded three examples of this. I have not written down the tablature for these tunes because the point is to show you how you can make up a phrase, then repeat it. Make up another phrase and repeat it. The "copy" of the first phrase need not be exact. Somewhat close is close enough. Just play freely within this loose structure of symmetry. As you continue to play, you will gradually develop an ear for this kind of playing. And before you know it, you will be creating your own tunes at a level far beyond your wildest imaginings!

The names of the three tunes demonstrating symmetry—

p149-1-E-SYMMETRY.mp3
p149-2-Fshrp-SYMMETRY.mp3

p149-3-Cshrp-SYMMETRY.mp3

-Chapter 14-

Finding Inspiration

SOURCES OF INSPIRATION: We can draw great inspiration from other flute players. Thanks to iTunes, all of the work these great players create are there for us to download. I have downloaded a fair share of these inspirational artists, and I often turn to my iPod, the digital player where I have these albums stored, for inspiration whenever I want it. All of the artists I name in this section are available on iTunes.

NATIVE AMERICAN FLUTE ARTISTS: **R. Carlos Nakai** is the man whom we can credit with making the Native American flute as popular as it is today. Albums to listen to are "Sanctuary", "Mythic Dreamer", "In Monument Valley", and "Changes". The albums I've named are flute without accompaniment. Many flute artists play with other musicians, probably to make their music more saleable. But I much prefer the lone flute with no others playing with the musician. Nakai has recorded albums with his own jazz quartet, as well as other musicians. He plays many kinds of music on the flute, and he has been the most important pioneer/explorer of this instrument. Nakai has even taken his flute to the concert stage and played with symphony orchestras. But for my taste and inspirational needs, I prefer the flute be played with no additional accompaniment, something Nakai does admirably well.

Mary Youngblood is another outstanding Native American flute artist. Her album, "The Offering", had a great influence on my own playing. On this album some of the tunes are played within a strict rhythm, just like those tunes at the beginning of this book, while some of the tunes are extemporaneous, played in the free-style, like those tunes we play in the last part of this book. That makes this album an excellent source of study for both styles.

SHAKUHACHI FLUTE ARTISTS: I am also inspired by shakuhachi players. This end-blown Japanese bamboo flute has a signature sound just like the Native American flute. There is no mistaking the sound of the shakuhachi. An excellent shakuhachi player is **Riley Lee**. Lee's work is very meditative, and I own several of his albums. My favorite Riley Lee album is titled, "Music for Zen Meditation". **John Neptune** is another excellent shakuhachi player. My favorite Neptune album is "WORDS CAN'T GO THERE", (yes, the title is in all uppercase). Neptune is a more aggressive player than most, but his work will show you what can be done with a simple folk flute like the shakuhachi.

All of these artists, as well as many others, often add background nature sounds. (Very meditative) In addition, some artists will heavily treat the sound of the flute until it loses all resemblance to the original. Sometimes that's good, and sometimes it's distracting. But fortunately we can listen to audio samples of all the albums sold on iTunes so we can decide if we like something before buying.

There are many download vendors that sell a wide variety of music. But Apple's iTunes has an eclectic range of music. This includes folk music and all kinds of ethnic music. That's why I prefer iTunes. Pandora and Spotify, among others, have this kind of music available as well. Brick and mortar stores that carry this kind of music are getting scarce, but Barnes and Noble still carries CDs for a wide variety of music, including music for the Native American flute as well as the shakuhachi.

PLAYING ALONG WITH NATURE SOUNDS: It's fun to extemporaneously play with a nature track while birds or thunderstorms are accompanying you. Listen to me play along with a thunderstorm in MP3 p153-Gpvc_StormSpirit.mp3. There is no TAB in the book for this tune. I played it on the fly. But I also played Corn Grinding Song along with birds in a rain forest, p153-E_CornGrindingSong_birds.mp3. (The TAB for Corn Grinding Song is on page 134.)

One way to get nature backgrounds is to buy them. But there's another option that won't cost you a dime. You can download all kinds of interesting sound backgrounds from FreeSound.org. This organization has thousands of tracks, and you will have great fun listening to audio samples on their site before downloading the ones you like. Thunderstorms, wind, whale calls, the ocean breaking on the beach, birds singing in a forest—all kinds of nature sound backgrounds are available from FreeSound.org. When you first visit, you have to set up your login info. But there's never an obligation, and you never have to pay. Just download what you want, then double-click the file to play it. Your resident MP3 player will automatically start playing the file. As it plays, play your flute along with it. You can use these sounds to make your own compositions, and you can even sell your work with no obligation to pay FreeSound.org. It's a good deal, and everybody wins. (I used files from this site to make a couple of the audio examples for this book.)

FLUTE CARE: Native American flutes are easy to take care of. If you own a wood flute, clean it with a soft, dry cloth. The finish the builder used should give it all the protection it needs. I would caution you to go easy with the furniture polish, if you find yourself inclined to go in that direction. If you get carried away, you might make the surface so smooth that the flute will be difficult to hold.

If the flute is bamboo, you might need to rub it down with tung oil every six months or so. Tung oil is an inexpensive oil that behaves like a finish. It seals the surface, and it dries like any standard furniture finish product. Tung oil actually slightly enhances the sound with each treatment.

PVC flutes are even easier to take care of. The flute is a high grade of plastic that requires no polishing. A soft cloth for an occasional wipe down is all you'll need.

FLUTE ACCESSORIES: If you are meditating at home and don't plan to take your flute anywhere, you won't have the need for a carrying **case**. But you will need one if you want to drive or bicycle somewhere with it. It wouldn't do to just put it on a carseat or strap it to your bike and drive away with it. You need to protect your investment. Flute cases come in various sizes and capacities. Some cases will hold several flutes. They are decorated in various ways, and some cases are very attractive. But even though the case will protect your flute, just the shock of transport might jar the block out of adjustment. Always be sure to check block placement when you take it out of the case. (page 31)

If you have three or four flutes, you will want to invest in a flute **rack**. These mount on the wall, and most of them hold the flutes horizontally. My flute rack holds five flutes, and it looks somewhat like the antler rack of a moose. Although I have more than five flutes, I put my five favorites on the rack and put the rest in a safe place for those occasional times I do play them. I bought my flute rack unfinished because it was cheaper. But you can also buy finished racks if you don't mind paying a bit more.

FLUTE MICS: If you want to perform with your flute, or if you want to play the flute for a large yoga class, you might want to amplify it. But you'll need a specific mic to fit a specific need.

Condenser Mics: A condenser mic is *omnidirectional.* This means it picks up sound from every direction. Suppose you are playing on a stage, and you have people behind you playing instruments. Or suppose you are playing for a yoga class, but the studio has traffic rolling by. A condenser mic might pick up that unwanted sound and interfere with the pure tone of your flute. This might not be objectionable in your particular situation. But then again it just might. Condenser mics are inexpensive, but they might not be what you want.

Dynamic Mics: A dynamic mic picks up sound from just one direction. Only the sound from the flute will be amplified. Dynamic mics are somewhat more expensive, but they are worth it if you want to total rule out unwanted sound. Their frequency range is somewhat limited, but those breathy sounds you sometimes produce while playing will not be amplified. They will be filtered out, leaving you with the pure sound of the flute. And while condenser mics are subject to feedback, something you absolutely don't want, dynamic flutes are not. So although condenser mics can be an expensive alternative, your best mic just might be a dynamic mic, regardless of application.

Where to Place the Mic: Intuitively one might think the mic would be placed at the end of the flute barrel, just like you would put a mic at the end of a trumpet or sax bell. But of course, this would be wrong. The sound is generated at the sound hole, not at the end of the barrel. And the mic, (flute mics are very small), is fastened to the barrel just below the sound hole. You might think that a very expensive mic is necessary, but it's not. You can pay a few thousand dollars for an expensive condenser mic, but that condenser mic might amplify all those unwanted sounds condenser mics are so famous for. Your best bet is to first try an inexpensive condenser mic. If it works, you've saved some bucks.

Flute Amps: The most popular amplifier for the Native American flute seems to be a unit called the "Roland Microcube". It weighs just 7 pounds and runs on either six AA batteries or a plugin power adapter. The unit is around $200, but its portability makes it worth the price. With this unit you can also plug in your iPod so you can play along with an audio background you might find at FreeSound.org. If you already own an amp, and if your flute mic has a 1/4" plug, you might try playing through the amp to see if you get a good sound. The Microcube has a frequency range mated to the Native American flute, but a guitar amp or keyboard amp might work just as well for you. Those amps might be much larger and heavier. But if this isn't an issue, it's worth giving your existing amp a try.

MAKING YOUR OWN FLUTE: Some people who enjoy working with wood will probably want to try making their own flute. There are kits you can purchase online that will challenge you to varying degrees. The simplest kit type is ideal for young kids. The flute is already made because it's a plastic flute. So there is no actual flute construction. But there's still a sense of accomplishment with kits like these because the fun part of the kit is the material you get with it to decorate it.

The next step up in flute kits is a flute that's already constructed but is left unfinished. This is a project for the more mature child or adult. Even though the wooden flute is already constructed, there is satisfaction in finishing it in your own way.

The most difficult flute kit is where the various parts are roughed out but you still have to do considerable work to make the flute presentable. In a kit like this there is significant handwork to be done. The most difficult part of this project will be to drill the note holes in the barrel and then tune the flute by elongating the holes until each note is in tune. Even if it's a kit where the holes are already drilled, there is no guarantee it will be in tune. Simply drilling the holes at the right spots won't give you an in-tune flute unless you are very, very lucky. So if you aren't a musician, or if you have trouble singing in tune, this project could be a disappointment. A few years back a well meaning relative made me a flute. But he didn't tune it because he knew he couldn't hear pitches correctly. Without telling my relative I had done so, I gave the flute to my friend, Chris Fuqua, the flute builder. It's quite a small flute, but he plugged all the holes, then redrilled and tuned them to make it a flute in the key of E. If you know someone who knows how to do this, building a flute from a kit at this level will work for you. You can finish it all up and then give it to someone who knows how to put the flute in tune. I have a very good sense of pitch. And I'm also skilled at woodworking. But I wouldn't tackle tuning a flute. That task is best left to those who truly know how.

CLOSING THOUGHTS: I put considerable thought into how I wanted to end this book because I want you to realize how important the Native American flute is, both as a World Music instrument and as a meditative tool. After years of playing the flute, I know that the sweet, deep music of this instrument is balm to the soul. With this profound fact well in mind, I was looking for a way to make this point, because I think it's the perfect way to sum up all the ideas in this book.

The Native American flute does not have a monopoly on meditative instruments. Any instrument, including the beauty of the human voice, can take us into a state of meditation. Have you heard the old Chinese proverb that says, "When the student is ready, the teacher will appear."? Apparently I was ready for the teacher to appear because my epiphany occured on a fogbound Sunday morning when I was well into my Feldenkrais routine. I was listening to NPR, (National Public Radio), Weekend Edition, and they were running a story about a young woman named Elizabeth LaPrelle. Elizabeth is one of a very small group of American singers who sings in the ornamental free style of the early Applachians. The old Scottish, Irish and English story-telling ballads go back hundreds of years, and Elizabeth sings these ballads in the fascinating free style of that period. Her voice is intense and haunting, and when she sings, she sounds far older than her 25 years. While listening to this story, I was startled at some of Elizabeth's comments about her music. The comments perfectly explain the kind of music I've tried to make available in this book, and I'm quite sure Elizabeth wouldn't mind me quoting her. Speaking about the characteristics of old Appalachian music, she said, "It doesn't have a lot of rhythm; it's free with meter; it has long, drawn-out phrases and lots of ornaments. So the ornaments are like the yip or trilling around the note—sliding up into the note instead of just stepping on it." (The "yip" she refers to is a combination of grace note and bark.)

What a perfect way of explaining the playing style of the extemporaneous free-style way of playing the Native American flute. We play long phrases, we slide into notes, we add ornaments like the Trill (warble), Hold, Raspberry, Grace note, and Bark. With this distinctive style we let our hearts play the flute rather than our heads. We tell beautiful stories with the flute, just as Elizabeth does with her old Appalachian melodies. Chris Fuqua, my good friend the flute builder, plays "Amazing Grace", just like Elizabeth sings it. (Listen to MP3 p159-Cshrp_AmazingGrace-Fuqua.) Chris doesn't play the tune with the rhythm it's constricted by in the typical church hymnal. He plays it freely. He adds ornamentation. He doesn't step on notes; he slides into notes. His heart, not his head, guides his fingers. Chris's treatment of this tune is included in the files you can download with the purchase of this book. And Elizabeth LaPrelle's style of singing is available from iTunes.

WITH AN ACCEPTING HEART: There is music inspiration everywhere you turn. All you need do is keep your ears open and your heart accepting. When you do this, the flute will take its own special place in your heart, and everyone around you will breathe with you as the beautiful meditative melodies pour out of your flute. If you play even the simplest tunes in this book, and if you put real passion into every note, the flute will transport you to that place of 'empty' joy where the stresses you live with will melt to nothingness, to emptyness, with each note you play.

So with that, I leave you to be inspired, to explore, to meditate, and to love all those within the reach of your heart.

The best of success with your flute playing.

Dick Claassen - author, composer, musician, teacher

Turn the page for download URL for free files→

Download *URL* and *PASSWORD* for the audio and video files

The audio/video files are FREE with this book. You can download them and then unzip them **with a password**. (Unzipping instructions for both Mac and PC are at the download page.)

Download all files at—

http://fluteflights.com/meditative-flute-DL

PASSWORD TO UNZIP ALL FILES—

Fg27r48P9bL

IMPORTANT: The password is not listed on the website. It's only in this book.

Help email: dick.fluteflights@gmail.com

Made in the USA
San Bernardino, CA
26 April 2015